THE SQUARE & COMPASS

A NEWMAN CENTURY

This book is dedicated to Stella and Raymond…

I am the landscape man

Limestone man

My bones are these stones

I'm Titanites giganteus

I'm Trigonia gibbosa

Liostrea

an oyster

I'm simply sea shells

Written & researched
Ilay Cooper

Illustrated & researched
Jack Daniels

Designed
James Twist

Published by The Square & Compass Books,
Worth Matravers, Swanage, Dorset BH19 3LF

To order copies please telephone 01929 439229

First published 2007

ISBN: 978-0-9555327-0-2

Where possible we have sought throughout this project to seek permissions for the wonderful illustrations contained within these pages. We will be happy to include any corrections or missing acknowledgements in any future reprints.

Set in Minion and URW Grotesk

Printed in Great Britain by The Friary Press, Dorchester, Dorset

Contents

Acknowledgements

Mr & Mrs Ray Aplin, Martin Ayres, Rob Besant, The Bournemouth Echo, Bishops of Swanage, Rhoda Bower, Ron Bower, Cath Bradshaw, Naomi Brooke (Mills), Penny Brooke, Chris & Nicola Brooker, Anthony Buffery, Brian Bugler, Hazel Bugler, John Burt, Valerie Butler, Nico Campbell-Allen, Jim Chambers, Karla Joy Cherryjackdaniels, Ian Ching, Nick Collis Bird, Lt Col Allan Cooper, Charles Cooper, David Critchlow, Victoria Cross, Nick Crutchfield, Dorset History Centre, Peter Du Cane, The English Stamp Company, Jim Etherington, Mike Etherington, Evangeline Evans (Banks), Sarah Foot (Loudoun), Nicky France, Joan Gillespie, John Gilson, Richard Green, Debbie Handy, John Hall, Dave Harris, John & Beryl Harris, David Haysom, Juliet Haysom, Treleven Haysom, Michael Holroyd, Colin James, Kevin Keates, Jo Lawrence, Sir Bernard Lovell, Marcus Lidell, Nick Mack, Matt4Frames, Ken & Molly Miller, Mary Newman, Bill & Marion Norman, Mark 'Nobby' Norman, Roger Peers, James Pembroke, Dr Bill Penley, Anne (Gainher) Powys-Lybbe, Reg & Esme Prior, David Pushman, Val & Di Quinn, Isabel Rawlins, Ann Richards, Tereska Roe, The Russell Coates Museum, Hugh Sandall, Sansom Gallery, Reg Saville, Marion Shaw, Alan Smith & Family, Elizabeth Smith, Gus Smith, Robert Smith, John Strange, Brian & Val Stumpe, Harry Tatchell, David Thomas, Diddy Thomas, James Twist, Tony Viney, Marjorie Wallace, the late Mary Spencer Watson, Andy Wells, Mrs Pat Welsh, Toby Wiggins, Tim & Wendy Wiggins, Vernon Young & Family; Susy Michie for editing, and a very special thanks to Gerald Corbett and to all those we've missed. This book would not have been possible without your help and co-operation.

OPPOSITE
Charlie Newman

Puddle Mill
Bradle
Wt. Orchard
Black Knowl
Lime Kiln
Linch Fm.
Brook
Tapershill
Westwood
Styles F.
Afflington F.
Woody Hyde
Downhays
Quarry Fm.
Kingston
Higher Down
Afflington Barn
Culverwell
Primrose Hill
Langton Matravers
Factory
Encombe House
Swyre Head
West Hill
Acton
Downshays Barn
Spyway Fm.
Bottom
Renscombe
Eastington
Worth Matravers
Weston
Freshwater
Encombe Pt.
Chapmans Pool
Emmit Hill
East Man
Seacombe Cliff
West Man
Winspit
Signal
St. Aldhelms or
St. Albans Head

Introduction

The Square & Compass, at Worth Matravers, presides over a three-point junction where the road from Corfe Castle meets the road from Swanage which runs onwards to St Aldhelms Head and Chapmans Pool. It overlooks every coming and going of the village. Since Charles Newman took over in March 1907, the Newman family have held the license. So March 2007 marks the Newman Centenary.

A pub is much more than a sum of its material parts. An attractive building helps, a beautiful view is a bonus, but it stands or falls on the community that feeds it, a mixture of landlord, staff, transitory folk and fixed clientele. As landlords, the Newmans dominate The Square story: Old Charlie & Florence, Eileen (and naughty Frank), Raymond & Stella, Raymond aided by his daughter, Mary, Young Charlie & Sarah, then Young Charlie with Kevin as manager. It is, after all, a Newman century. Everyone who enters this pub adds to its atmosphere. Many staff and punters appear haphazardly in this book: most are missing.

The Landlord

Traditionally, The Square was a man's club. Triumphs and tragedies, the daily grind, were punctuated with beer and spirits. Wives and children continued their lives below and disapproving Methodists set up their chapel next door. Fuelled by the Fear of God, church or chapel frowned over the community, gathering up young and old of a Sunday, each in his best clothes.

The Preacher

The pub was the church's antithesis, condemned from the pulpit as ungodly. At best, it was an escape from the household, a place of relaxation where men met to converse, plan, exchange local news or play indoor games. It was the valve on the pressure cooker. At worst, it introduced alcoholism and gambling to blight men's lives.

The Square expanded, altered and, faced with social change, adjusted. During the Newman century, women – not local women, but arty, racy outside women – slipped in, then assumed their rightful place. The Newman masterstroke was inactivity. When plush and plastic invaded other Purbeck pubs, The Square stayed implacably the same. Folk suggested money-spinning innovations: successive Newmans listened and ignored. If their reaction was negative, it had positive results.

When we were boys, in the fifties, Worth was a living village, a bit grubby, with a pump to fill our water bottles, two shops and families living in almost every cottage. Old men sat near the pond yarning. Few households boasted a car. That was crucial.

Jack Daniels at the pump, 1965

Ilay Cooper at the pub, 1978

Men went to work on sit-up-and-beg black bicycles, each with lunch in his war-surplus khaki rucksack. Agriculture mechanised, quarries closed. Work within range of that bicycle declined.

The rural world faded, the city boomed. Worth folk quit for larger towns in the face of unemployment. Their homes became promising investments, escapes from London, a good place to retire. Humble cottages became tidy, manicured residences well beyond their aspirations. The community died, the chapel closed, the church congregation withered. Dark at night, Worth became a place with a past, but no future.

The Square and Compass weathered Worth's transition, into an era where everyone (well, almost everyone) lives in a car, where distances have shrunk. Under Newman rule, alone of village institutions, it has flourished into modern times.

★

I first entered The Square in 1961, carol-singing through a still-living village. Then, Worth's working men formed the clientele, diluted in summer with a dash of professional folk or adventurous holidaymakers exploring Purbeck. Sixties Worth had lost its pre-war flavour.

Generally, I drank in Swanage, at pubs rising and falling on fickle fashion but, after days bird watching or fishing, we would visit some favourite village pub. There were several: The Fox in Corfe, the then-modest Scott Arms, a stuffed Hen Harrier beside its bar, The King's Arms in Langton and The Square and Compass. Settling in Worth parish, I stuck with The Square but, often abroad, became a migrant not a fixture. Few folk from the 1960s still turn up. Many are dead or moved away; some have given up social drinking.

Jack Daniels approached the pub quite differently. Born a 'Brummie' kid in 1963, he came to Purbeck for most holidays. So, in the mid 1970s, he often sat outside or in the children's room after suffering the coastal walk from the lighthouse. His grandparents had recommended Swanage, where his parents bought a holiday home. There he settled in 1986, as a semi-retired Punk and from there he studied photography. For him, The Square became an obsession.

Jack suggested a book to celebrate the Newman century. Charlie and Mary Newman were enthusiastic. I agreed to research and write it. Inevitably, our roles sometimes overlapped. Jack did some research, especially on the internet, and I provided and took some photographs.

The building and its origin

The first Charlie Newman placed The Square and Compass firmly in the 13th century, thereby impressing 'foreign' punters, who valued antiquity. That is not ancient around Worth. Few know better than the current Charlie Newman how richly the area is scattered with Roman and pre-Roman settlements and artefacts.

Mediaeval Worth huddled into the little hollow below the church, its cottages fashioned of wood and clay, but The Square was raised in the mid 18th century, born of the Age of Reason. Strong and confident, it sits up high, facing into the prevailing gales, built open and exposed in an era when ghoulies and ghosties were in retreat. Its prominent situation at the crossroads suits an inn, but was it built or chosen as such?

Samuel Donne's 1772 map of Worth, commissioned after William Calcraft bought the village, is the earliest evidence of the building's existence. Donne depicts it as a simple elongated rectangle labelled 'Litchard Bank'. Mr Voss's 1840s map calls it 'Bank'. Together, they destroy a myth, perhaps created by Old Charlie.

Early print by Edwin Charles Pascoe Holman RWS, gifted to Hazel Bugler by Joan Begbie

The pub was called Bank, he explained, because it served as a bank for local quarrymen, the publican exchanging beer or cash for tooled stone paving. There are references to that happening. When a landlord was in the stone industry, stone cutters from nearby could bring him paving in return for credit. An old photograph shows the resultant stack of paving outside The Black Swan in Swanage. In Worth, however, 'Bank' described the steep slope onto the sunken track. Litchard Bank stresses this interpretation: 'Litchard' stems from the same root as 'lynchet', a roadside bluff, a topographical sort of bank. So if Bank Bank ever functioned as a bank, it had nothing to do with the name.

Worth village sits below St Nicholas of Myra

1772 Donne map

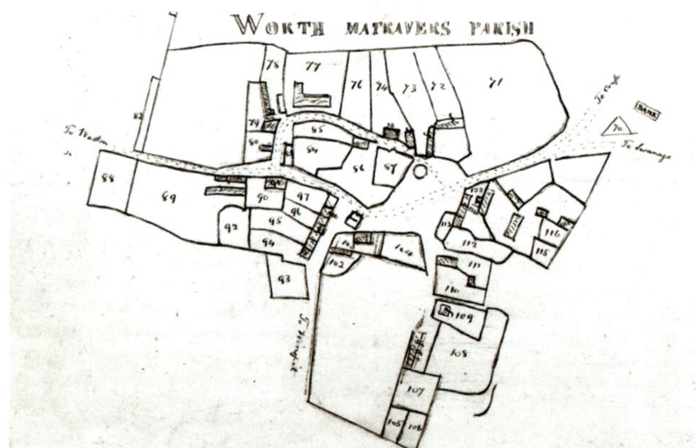

1840s map by Voss, marking Bank

Quarrymen at Sheepslights, c1926

The building held a tiny strip of land, perhaps merely right of access across its front and a small garden at the rear. The triangle of land in front, where the pub sign now stands, was bought by the brewer in August 1920 from Captain Marston in the notorious Worth sale. Marston, heir to the Calcraft Estate, was a man with mysterious debts. Some say he was addicted to gambling, others that he was subject to blackmail. Either way, after inheriting, he sold Rempstone Estate south of the chalk ridge. A shrewd Bournemouth businessman, P. M. Bright, bought Worth, then sold it in smaller lots. At that second sale, in July 1922, Strong's bought the triangular plot behind The Square.

In the absence of clear records, a structure records its own history. The Square was built as two cottages facing approximately southwards, the western one being larger. There are several clues to that division. The single massive wall across its axis, between the corridor and the Big Room, divided the two unequal parts. The façade betrays two front doors and a lost window. The window west of the porch, clashing with the symmetry, was once a doorway. Great slabs from East Man, the hill east of Winspit valley, created that porch in the 19th century and at its west side are traces of the lost window. Between the porch and the eastern window is a blocked doorway into the smaller cottage. Perhaps the builder wanted to house his parents.

Later, a lean-to bar was added to the back, with hatches pierced through the original rear wall. The bar door was once a back door. Other, wooden internal divisions changed with time. The partition between the corridor and the stair-well is old, since the corridor paviors retain chisel-marks, worn off the rest of the floor. The wooden partition beside the corridor to the museum was added later, smoothed paviors passing beneath it. Here, marks in the stone suggest two lost doorways across the axis of the building.

The museum wing creates a T plan of the original rectangle. It has an odd gable, a parapet protecting tiles from the wind, and contrasts with the older section, the rooms and roof being higher. Probably, this was built around 1850; perhaps the cottages were combined and the stone slab porch added simultaneously. This new wing, with a separate stairwell, became the landlord's domain, the museum section being the living room with a cooking range. In the mid 1970s, its south end was partitioned off for a children's room.

A young Charlie on the parapet above the children's room

Showing carpenter's tools

The orginal Oxford Blue…

The current sign by Al Bowerman

Regular visitors now in their nineties say that The Square has hardly changed since they reached up to buy ginger beer at the counter-door, although 'clutter' has built up on top of the porch and in front of the pub. Old photographs show the facade remarkably austere. A long sign 'Strong Romsey Ales and Spirits' used to run across the façade above the porch. Later, to the right of the porch, another, white on navy, read 'The Square & Compass'. Old Charlie introduced the fuchsia bush against the west end of the façade and cherished it, giving away cuttings. When it died in the bitter winter of 1947, he replanted it from a cutting he'd put in the cemetery. Not far from it, incised in a paving stone, the letters ACRIB have a mysterious significance, revealed to few.

As far back as there are pictures, an inn sign stood on the triangle of land in front. In early Newman times, it bore only the name of the pub, white on navy. Previously, when few folk read, there must have been a picture sign. One was re-established in the late 1960s, inaccurately showing the tools of a carpenter, lying on a block of stone. This was followed by a stylised set of mason's tools painted buff on an Oxford Blue ground (Jack Daniels cherishes both of these signs).

Lodging guests must have been minor business during the 18th and 19th centuries. Who would have come? There was little tradition of holidays in the country and most visitors to Worth stayed with those they had come to see. What was the 19th century layout of the interior? Probably the Parlour housed customers, leaving the rest of the ground floor to the family. When the Newmans took the lease in 1907, there were three licensed rooms: the bar, the Tap Room and the Parlour. The Square relied on a small, regular clientele of farming folk and quarrymen. There were few unfamiliar faces.

The Parlour was extended into the stable block. A 1935 photograph of Naomi Brooke (then Mills) and her sister shows the chimney above the gable of the main building. Naomi recalls the cramped little Parlour, where the guests took their meals. Leon Heron's 1936 cartoon in the Tap Room puts that chimney on the single storey stable block. That dates the expansion and explains a large photograph in the Big Room. Captioned 'Reconstruction by Hayter and Son. The Builders of Swanage. November 1935', it shows Old Charlie sitting with Leslie Banks, behind them, Judge Jellinek. Hayter, the builder, saw an advertising opportunity. In accepting the picture, Old Charlie fell for it! They replaced the solid eastern wall of the ground floor with a rolled steel joist, boxed in with timber as a rather-too-regular Olde

Worlde Beam. The fireplace was reconstructed in the new end wall. It commemorates the end of an era: horses, thus stables, were defunct. A little stretch of cobbles, the entrance to the cobbled stable, remains near the lavatories.

Richard Cardell's 1937 poem covers the Parlour's expansion: 'Reincarnated from the barn, the lounge is worth a call…' Then, 'the tap room was a larder once…' If one is accurate, why not the other? The Tap Room had been changed recently enough for someone to know its original use. It holds much of The Square's charm. Its ugly, stone fireplace, built in the fifties to replace a harshly-pointed brick one, was swept away in 1990 to reveal the original inglenook and a bread oven. The décor is dominated by Heron's cartoon, showing Old Charlie at closing time.

'Got to be cruel to be kind!'
Old Charlie by Leon Heron, 1936

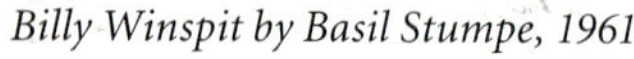
Billy Winspit by Basil Stumpe, 1961

Charlie James Newman by Leon Heron, c. 1936

Jo Lawrence, who drank here often from the 1930s, praises it as a wonderful likeness. On the other side of the doorway is another Heron caricature of Old Charlie's doomed son, another Charlie, in a flat cap, beside a 1977 photograph showing his landlady sister, Eileen, shaking hands with his landlord son, Raymond. On the east wall is a large photograph of the Sunday crowd outside the pub in 1939 and by it a Purbeck grub plaque, provided by Bill Norman and Colin Lander, to celebrate the Newmans' 70th anniversary. Not far from it is a perforated-zinc spyhole; from the stairs, one can slide back a wooden panel to see, unseen. On the table below is barely decipherable WWII graffiti.

Raymond Newman used to preserve dead animals and birds, injecting them with formaldehyde; in the window recess a glass case contains a squirrel and a hedgehog.

Between windows is a portrait of Billy Winspit, a loyal customer and famous local character, which the painter, Basil Stumpe, gave to Eileen in the late sixties. Then, everyone complained at its jarring brightness, but forty years of nicotine calmed the colours, then obscured the image. On the other window sill is a stone cat, made by the present Charlie. Carved reliefs in the fire recess depict the Aga Khan in a top hat, his horse 'Mahmoud', 1936 Derby winner and a portrait of Old Charlie with, written above him, 'Beer is Best' and below, 'New Man'. Some of these were by Kytie Harris, famous locally for his 'Asbestos Man', a huge Portland Stone figure created during the late 1930s as logo for a company manufacturing fireproof asbestos suits. Among the metal pans, pressing irons and hammers is a portrait of a tabby cat. Even that has a story: Raymond, bidding at an auction at Wareham, ended up with the wrong lot – a stack of cat pictures. The tabby, the least pernicious, is a monument to caution. The Salter spring-balance was bought to weigh pumpkins on Pumpkin Day, but it has been superseded by events, since it only measures up to 600lbs.

The Big Room, less sympathetic, is dominated by the mock Tudor panelling, false beam and parquet floor of the 1935 alterations. The stone fireplace holds a generous log fire in winter. The hatch nearest the door served the original little Parlour. The large hatch looking towards the fireplace, Stella Newman's idea, was opened around 1978. On its side is a shelly piece of spangle worked by Brian Bugler, inscribed to commemorate the 70th Newman anniversary. Above it, a portrait of a kipper was painted for Raymond by his friend, Eric Bunny. Between hatches is the large photograph donated by Hayters and in the corner beyond are some imaginative posters by Ian Ching, advertising the earliest Square Fairs. The propeller, I found whilst swimming under Gad Cliff. The painted sign, 'The Jolly Landlord and the Mad Dog', has a story...

Much of the furniture came from auctions at Cottees in Wareham, but some features on the previous landlady's list in 1907, like the table by the door. Its unlocked drawer held a gold sovereign, recovered from a 1922 wreck in the Bay of Biscay, which disappeared during Eileen's reign. The eccentric driftwood chair, more comfortable than it looks, was made by Nick Crutchfield. There has been a piano here as long as anyone remembers. For a while there were two, but, one Burn's Night, the battered, tuneless one was ejected down the steep track to its dissonant doom. Occasionally, pianists turn up. Mostly it is just 'Chopsticks'.

The Aga Khan

The Aga Khan's horse, Mahmoud

Old Charlie

Old Charlie by John Doust, ARPS

Kytie Harris with his 'Asbestos Man' – Bell's Asbestos saved many lives with their fire proofing

Above the mantelpiece is a 1949 photograph of Old Charlie by John Doust, between a drawing of Augustus John by the cartoonist, Low (creator of Colonel Blimp) and a portrait of Old Charlie by John. The cats in the fireplace were carved by Billy Winspit – William Jeremiah Bower – of the Tap Room portrait, who lived in Winspit Cottage until his death in 1966. The cat in the window is another by the present Charlie.

Stumpe's portraits either side of the fireplace window depict three generations of landlords – Old Charlie Newman, Eileen, Raymond and a regular customer, George Bugler. Beside them is a selection of photographs of Raymond and a portrait by Carol Bugler. Leslie Ward, a prominent local artist and a customer between the wars, drew the view of Swanage Mill Pond. Near it is Cardell's poem and a neat little pen drawing of three fishermen in a clinker-built 'stone barge' by Tony Buffery, a geologist and regular visitor since the early 1960s.

George Bugler by Basil Stumpe

George Crane's coloured photograph, near the window, is of the musicians, Keith and Marcia Pendlebury, whom Young Charlie met in Cork in 1993. They joined the many musicians who have played here. A black and white photograph shows Old Charlie rigged for an early television appearance in 1938. It is signed by Elizabeth Cowell, one of the first woman presenters.

Behind the bar, with only the slightest glance towards reality, hang two bats created by Karen Lyttle before she married and fled to New Zealand. Karla, coming the other way, married Jack and made it quits.

The Big Room by Tereska Roe

Worth drinking? The early days

To start at the beginning… but where is the beginning? The Dorset History Centre at Dorchester holds the Ale House Recognizances, 18th century account books recording licensed drinking places. It was all so simple. The Square, according to rumour, was previously 'The Sloop', earlier still, 'The Two Hammers'. Just look it up.

Under Worth Matravers, in the 1752 book, the first giving alehouse names, comes 'The Two Hammers' (oddly, in later registers, 'The Three Hammers'), held by Edward Smith. Smith's occupation was blacksmith. Reg Saville mentioned that smithies often housed an adjoining alehouse. The smithy, always heated by its forge, was generally manned, since the craft relied on unexpected accidents as much as planned custom. In later registers, Smith features as a 'victualler', a title rightly belonging to his wife, who served food when necessary. Then, a woman had little existence in law outside the rank and occupation of her spouse; in reality, she was his 'other half'.

After John Calcraft's death in 1772, Bridget, whom he had secretly married at eighteen, then abandoned, emerged to claim a wifely share of his estates. A document was drawn up in 1777, listing his lands and tenants. There, sure enough, is Edward Smith, paying three shillings and fourpence for a house and shop. He features in the alehouse registers from 1738, presumably already trading under the sign of Two Hammers. His was not the only alehouse in Worth Parish. From 1733 to 1744 Edward Haskell held licenses to sell ale and brandy, probably at Quarr Farm, where some Haskells were established. Thomas Dover had held The Rose since 1733 and his widow briefly took over after his death in 1762. The Rose was a one-up, one-down cottage standing below the pond, opposite London Row and enlarged into Happy Cottage after 1923.

Why were there so many alehouses in mid-18th century Worth? The village thrived on two industries, agriculture and stone quarrying. With farming, the early and mid 18th century was 'business as usual'. Quarrying, however, saw a boom. Until the early 18th century the main source of stone was the Purbeck beds around Langton and Swanage, yielding valuable paving and tile, but interest in cliffstone was growing. In the mid 18th century a huge project was launched to enclose Ramsgate

Schedule the third referred to Marked No. 3

Tenants Names

Henry Jenkins Millcroft

Joseph Luther – part of Mathew Benfield's

Elias Benfield – Ditto

Stoborough – Giles Brown – Tan yard

Copyholders Rents in Worth } Jn. Smith – Woodgate Tenement

Edward Smith, House and Shop

Jn. Benfield – Jn. Benfield's Tenemt.

Leasehold Rents

Barwell

Tho:

Detail from the Dower of Bridget Calcraft, 1777

harbour with a mole. This demanded vast amounts of readily-transportable stone. Purbeck's cliff-stone ('Purbeck Portland') block could be lowered into boats and carried on prevailing winds up the Channel directly to the work-site. Between June 1750 and September 1752, Purbeck contributed 15,000 tons of cliffstone to the Ramsgate project; between January 1764 and January 1771, a further 94,000 tons. New cliff quarries were opened, creating dramatic coastal features, which later drew several generations of visitors to Worth. Today, such quarries are air-brushed away at enormous cost, in the interests of Environment, Health and Safety. Then, the country still moved forward.

Worth was well placed for cliff quarries at Seacombe, Winspit and St Aldhelms Head. On the west side of the Head there was even a stone pier, reached by a track running down Pier Bottom, for loading boats. Workers moved in to serve the demand and merchants came to check progress. They needed somewhere to eat and drink. Smuggling also prospered.

No alehouse license was granted in Worth between 1764 and 1770; damp destroyed the later registers. It is hard to imagine the parish as a dry area. Smith still held a shop, presumably the smithy, but was he serving beer?

Then the story becomes complicated. Donne's 1772 map depicting numbered plots, shows the borders of Downshay Farm running across the front of The Square building, placing it in Downshay, not Worth village as defined by the 1771 sale to Calcraft. Smith was a Calcraft tenant, thus that building could not have housed 'The Two Hammers'! Donne also listed the tenants beside the numbers of the plots they held. Edward Smith's house and shop was at Church Cottage, next to the church tower, an improbable site for either a blacksmith's or an alehouse. Smith, whose uncle was a direct ancestor of Stella Smith/Newman, died in 1779 aged 70. Later, the terrace known as Pond View included a blacksmith's shop, traces of a forge surviving in the smallest cottage.

Records for Downshay Farm specifically mention, but don't locate, a pair of cottages held in 1771 by John Toop 'and another'. Were they the cottages later combined to form a new public house? The only hint of a Toop connection with the alehouse business is that a William Toop offered surety for Smith when he renewed his license in 1753. Often, men involved with the liquor trade gave surety to one another.

A list of 'things to do', dated September 1771 and drawn up by John Bishop, Clavell's estate manager, includes this note: 'Public House in Worth to be fixed and Justices applied to… NB Bishop to go to Clavell'. Clavell was a local magistrate. Having just bought Worth Manor and commissioned Samuel Donne to map it, John Calcraft set about other legal tasks relating to his new manor. Establishing a public house was one such task, but there is no evidence that it was done.

At the valuation of Downshay Farm, before its sale to Thomas Hyde in 1776, Toop held 'a substantial built cottage' at £5 a year, the same rent that the first certain Square landlord, Joseph Cox, was paying in 1792. Since there is no mention in that valuation of a public house, it can't have existed in the present building in 1776. The public house license, and its separation from the rest of the farm, might date from 1776, when Thomas Hyde, who already had brewing interests in Wareham, bought Downshay. 1786 may also be significant: that year John Toop died. Joseph Cox was probably in the building, running a public house, by 1790. Did Toop's death create the vacancy he filled?

Two 1790s documents establish the present building as a public house. 'The Western Flying Post or Sherbourne & Yeovil Mercury and General Advertiser' of Dec 5th 1792 announced an auction to be held at The Red Lion in Wareham. Listed as Lot 5 is… 'All that well accustomed Freehold Public-House, or Inn, called the Sloop, with the garden, stable, and out-houses thereto adjoining and belonging, situated in the parish of Worth Matraverse aforesaid, in the occupation of Joseph Cox, as a yearly tenant, at £5 per annum, and heretofore taken out of Downshay Farm, aforesaid.' Thomas Hyde, a Poole merchant, overstretched himself. The French Revolution of 1789 and threat of war ruined him. This was a bankruptcy sale.

Hyde had invested heavily in Purbeck's clay mining, supplying Josiah Wedgwood. By 1771 he, along with a butcher, 'directed' a brewery in Pound Lane, Wareham, where he also owned several inns. Presumably, they acquired this brewery from Thomas Phippard and Giles Brown, another butcher, who owned it in 1753. Hyde bought Downshay in 1776, so had every reason to encourage the opening of an inn in the two strategic cottages in Worth.

At the auction, William Calcraft bought Downshay Farm for Rempstone Estate. The Sloop was sufficiently flourishing to attract Thomas Phippard, again a brewer in Wareham. He bought lot 5, a purchase confirmed by a massive deed held by Charlie Newman. We spent five hours transcribing the legalese that surrounds the meat: '…at a sale… of the Estates of the said Thomas Hyde… Thomas Phippard was the best bidder for the public house or Inn now or ever called the Sloop… now occupied by Joseph Cox situated in the parish of Worth Matravers…'

A document in Dorchester confirms this is the present pub. Dated 26th April 1833, when it passed from Thomas Phippard to Samuel Townsend, it is described as: '…all that messe tenement or public House or Inn ('lately' inserted) commonly called or known by the name or sign of the Sloop ('but now The Square and Compass' inserted)… late… occupied by Joseph Cox and now by Charles Bower situate in the parish of Worth Matravers… .'

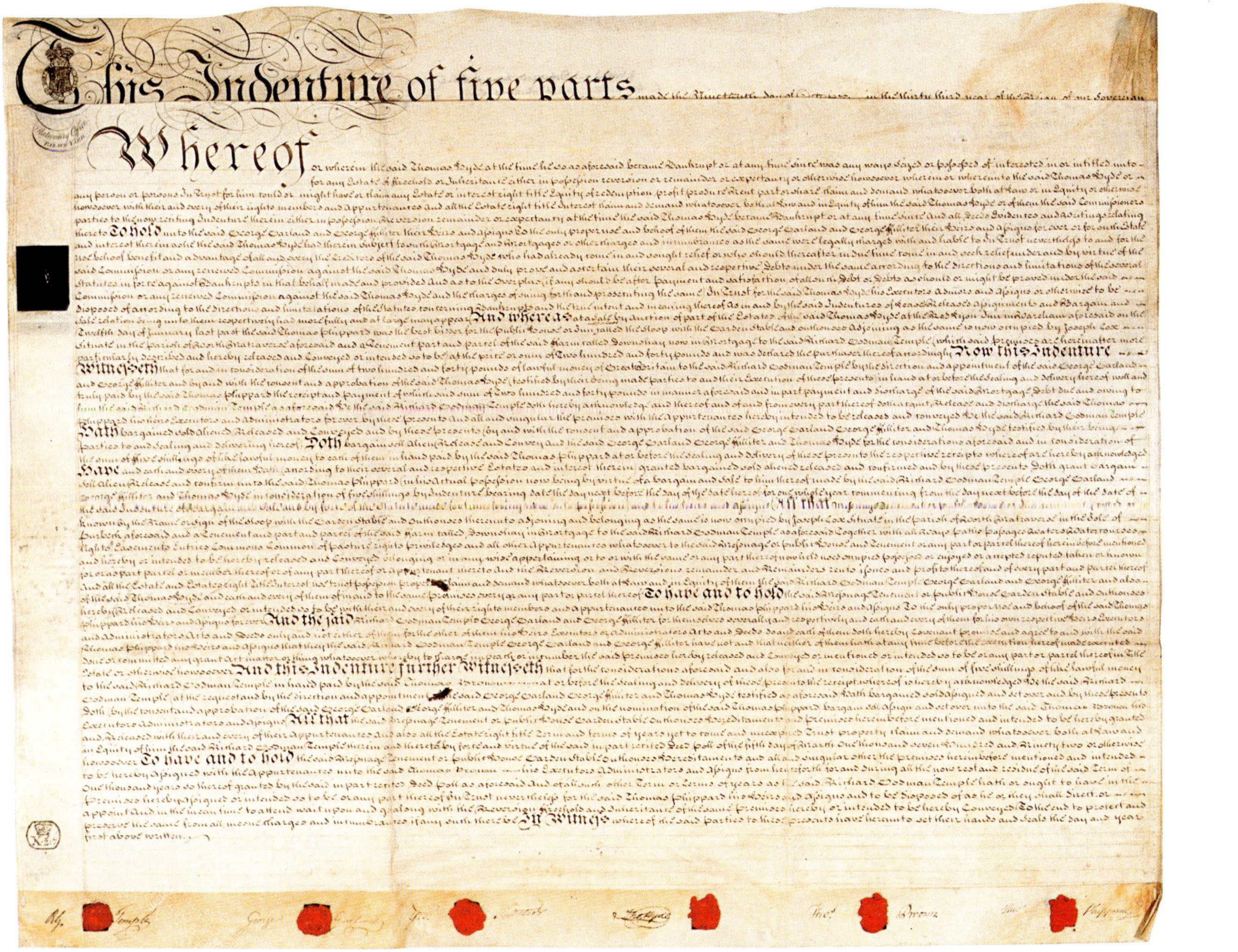

The 1793 deed confirming Thomas Phippard's purchase of the pub, mentioning The Sloop and Landlord Joseph Cox

uses into possn & to his heirs All that messe tenement or public House
or Inn lately commonly called or known by the name or sign of the Sloop
but now the Square & Compass
with the garden stable & outhouses thereunto adjoining & belonging as the
same late was occupied by Joseph Cox and now by Chas Bower situate in the parish of
Worth Purbeck

Document confirming the sale of The Square and Compass, formally The Sloop, to Samuel Townsend from Thomas Phippard

The beauty of this document is that the words 'lately' and 'but now The Square and Compass' (never, from the beginning 'Compasses'!) were added in a contrasting reddish ink. It is signed and dated in that same ink. The change of name presumably came with Charles Bower taking over. (Over the years, the pub was to show a 'Charles' proclivity.) Edward Smith, the blacksmith, called his alehouse Two Hammers after tools of his trade. Bower was a stonecutter, so squares and compasses were amongst his tools. Who was the seaman who named The Sloop? Toop of the Sloop? The answer may lie amongst the documents in Dorchester. It evaded me.

Was Joseph Cox, first certain landlord of The Sloop, related to Samuel Cox of Winfrith, also an innkeeper? A Langton man, Cox's first mention in Worth records is his marriage to Betty Coastfield, daughter of a well-established villager, in April 1787. She died the following year after bearing a son. Cox then married Temperance Corben at Langton in 1789 and she bore at least three children, all christened at Worth. Cox may have settled in The Sloop around the time of his first marriage. He appears regularly in the Parish Overseers Accounts between 1791 and 1810, submitting unspecified bills, always under £1, for Church work. That for 1810 seems to be for mending a lock. He died in Langton in October 1834 aged 83. Nothing more fleshes him out.

Nothing, save remnants and a silver shilling in the museum, certainly connects the building with the disastrous wreck of the Halsewell of January 6th 1786, in which 168 people died. There is a tenuous link: George Garland, a Poole merchant who signed the 1793 Sloop deed, presumably as a creditor of Hyde's, was then tenant at Eastington Farm, a few fields from the pub. Worth's vicar, Mr Morgan Jones, records 'I was sitting at breakfast with Mr Garland on Friday the 6th of January, when news

was brought, that a large ship was on the shore. The disposition of the country to plunder is well known; we therefore immediately mounted our horses, to afford what protection we could to the unfortunate. You remember Winspit Quarry; she was lost half a mile to the east of it....'

Garland played a major role in the rescue and was presented with a tea service in recognition. Some of the 82 survivors must have lodged in The Sloop, whether or not it was already an inn. A reference to George III visiting the site of the wreck in 1789 led me to fantasies of His Majesty pausing in his ride to sit on the wall and quench his thirst. He was not above such things. No such luck: he sailed past from Weymouth in a naval vessel.

Other events must have stirred Worth folk. The French Revolution and, from 1793, the resulting war called in troops and militia to man coastal defences. Allied German troops marched across South Dorset. Innkeepers were expected to accommodate troops and suffered if they refused. In 1859 Henry Cake, landlord of The Kings Arms in Stoborough, was fined £1 for refusing to put up two soldiers of the 13th Huzzars 'on the march through Wareham'. Few marched through Worth.

In 1803, the height of invasion fears, militia must have manned guns at Battery Corner and also Powder House, the small, rapidly-decaying battery under Hounstout that guarded Chapmans Pool. A cannon from that period remained at the end of Pier Bottom when we were boys, perhaps protecting the approach from that elusive pier. Men in uniform stopping for a drink would have set the village talking. And the victory of Waterloo in 1815, how was that marked at The Sloop?

An alehouse was a modest affair, a room set aside for serving drink. An inn was altogether bigger, providing food and lodging. The Sloop was the only inn in Worth, if not the only licensed house. Two men, Joseph Green (in 1813 & '16) and George Barnes (in 1821), describe themselves as 'innkeeper' in the register of Worth baptisms. In August 1819, Barnes charged the Parish for '...Beer for Jurymen when John Corbin's Son was killed.' Did Cox retire to Langton around 1810, giving way to Green, then Barnes? Was he only mentioned in the 1833 deed because his name appeared in the 1793 one? Charles Bower, described as 'innkeeper' in 1827, was certainly landlord of The Square. But in January 1831, Calcraft, when dealing with the Wareham brewer, Thomas Phippard's Purbeck Estate, paid George Barnes £5 3 0d and Joseph Green £1 13 0d. So, if they are dealing in alcohol, these men overlap Charles Bower.

Between 1750 and 1840, with a strange peak of Anglo-French cooperation in 1800-10 during the Napoleonic War, smuggling was an important Purbeck trade; cliff quarrymen, fishermen and coastal trading vessels were almost all involved. With duties often over 100%, few saw the trade as disreputable. At one side of the Channel tea and port wine cost four times the price asked on the other. Brandy was cheap at only twice the price. In 1783, a sloop called 'Orestes', patrolling the Purbeck coast, caught a boat laden with tea off St Aldhelms Head. A large cutter opened fire in her defence, killing one naval man and injuring two more.

An entry in the Swanage Rector's diary describes another battle in 1827 at St Aldhelms Head. 80 smugglers under Mr Lucas, innkeeper of The Ship in Wool, fought 10 Preventive Men and two smugglers were killed. Young Charlie, in his forays over the fields at the Head, discovered several musket balls, perhaps left from such skirmishes between smugglers, fresh-landed, and excise-men lying in wait.

Stories always change with time. One tells of a warning shot, fired towards a boat under the Head in 1834, accidentally hitting the bowman. He was said to be connected with The Square and Compass, where they carried him to die. The Dorset County Chronicle of Thursday 6th November 1834 puts it differently: 'On Sunday evening an affray took place at St Albans Head, in Purbeck, between some smugglers and the Preventive force, when Bishop, a man from the neighbourhood of Dorchester, received a wound in the neck, which it is feared will prove fatal, as he is unable to be removed from a small public house at Worth Matravers, where he was removed after receiving the injury; it appears that he fired a pistol in the air on coming into contact with the Preventive Party, which one of the men immediately returned...' In 1834, a row of cottages was built at the Head to house the coastguards and excisemen set to stem the flow of contraband. They became frequent customers at The Square.

Did England's greatest painter call at The Sloop in September 1811? Judging by his sketch-books, Turner crossed Poole Harbour and landed at Wytch, then walked or rode to Corfe, probably putting up at The Greyhound. He continued to Swanage over Nine Barrow Down and, from Durlston, sketched the two bays. His next drawings show Corfe from Kingston, but his accompanying (dreadful) verse talks of St Aldhelm's Head and the Halsewell wreck. Surely, a call at the nearest inn... .

If Charles Bower held the lease in 1833, Samuel Townsend, 'Common Brewer', of Wareham owned The Square. It passed to Pantons, brewers in Ringwood, Wareham

and Swanage, who became 'H.J. Panton & Co'. The widow of one of the Pantons, who was the daughter of the painter William Frith, brought the family a last burst of fame in 1909, when she published 'Fresh Leaves and Green Pastures'. Telling too much of Purbeck Society, it was suppressed since it was claimed to libel Captain Marston. Elizabeth Kittoe, the remarried widow of the other partner, sold the brewery to Charles and David Faber in 1893. David Faber had bought up several breweries in Romsey during the 1880s, amalgamating them under the banner of 'Thomas Strong & Co', a company founded in 1858. So Strongs came to own The Square. But Worth was 'a distant land of which we know little', and, as long as the rent came in, the brewers left The Square alone.

Charles Bower was born in Acton: by mistake, in a census, he put the hamlet as the parish of his birth. The 1841 census lists him as a Publican, aged 41, married to Martha, 36, both from Langton Matravers. Martha was a Phippard, as was the earlier owner of The Sloop. Was there any connection? All their nine children, born between 1826 to 1847, were christened in Worth. In 1851 Bower described himself as Mason/Publican; probably he was a stonecutter by day, leaving Martha to run the inn, a common pattern. While women did the donkey-work, men were the face the world saw.

Oddly, the Bowers give Young Charlie another connection with the pub. Their daughter, Martha, married George Stickland but died three years later, probably in childbirth. He married again, his daughter being grandmother to Stella Smith, Young Charlie's mother. Charles Bower's son, also Charles, married Sarah Smith of Worth, probably another tie with Stella.

Victoria reigned over a rigidly-divided society. The 19th century working populace of Worth was divided between stone-cutters, agricultural workers and outsiders employed as coastguards and excisemen. The latter formed a surprisingly high proportion until 1840, then declined. Their entry into the pub probably inspired the exit of other customers, some seeing a chance to act unnoticed. The romance of village life was observed from afar by the middle classes. Walking to enjoy the countryside was rare; there were few hikers amongst the clientele and Sundays brought in the same folk as the rest of the week. But when the Wilde sisters presented a lectern to Worth church in 1874, they mentioned 'holiday connections' with the village.

The Upper Orders, on hunting or shooting expeditions, may have stopped for a drink. In Spring, they shot at the breeding puffins, razorbills and guillemots circling off the cliff; they made nice targets with their fast, direct flight. Fishermen collected the corpses for bait. The Square was an ideal halt on such outings. Folk hunting, more usefully, for foxes or game birds stopped by, as do fishermen and anglers today.

The Court Registers of Wareham Petty Sessions from 1844 to 1869 reveal no dirt on The Square, probably more due to Worth's isolation than to its chastity. Town pubs had neighbours behind lace curtains, ready to complain as drunken men invaded the street. In Worth, who, apart from the vicar and Methodists, would rock the boat? Most crime affected the landowning magistrates: poaching, trespassing 'in pursuit of conies' or other game, using a greyhound for game, hawking or fishing without a license. In season, there was the scrumping of apples or turnips.

John Smith and family gravestone

Alcohol-related crimes include a single case of smuggling as late as 1851, when the Champ brothers 'unshipped 70 gallons of Brandy' in Swanage. Drunk driving is not new: in 1845 Thomas Talbot of Worth was fined a shilling 'for returning home with a Team (of horses) in liquor.' Had he been 'up The Square'? William Craft, who painted amazing naïve pictures of Swanage, was several times in trouble for drunkenness which led to 'assault and beating'.

In the late 1850s several drunks were sentenced to five or six hours in the stocks 'in default of distress'. From 1866, there were fines for refusing to leave an alehouse when ordered by the landlord or a constable. Selling liquor without a license occurred frequently. In 1845, the Langton Innkeeper, Thomas Stevens, was fined six shillings for assault. Other offences by landlords included possession of faulty measures, 'keeping an inn disorderly', allowing drunkenness and, above all, not observing the correct hours. Often, there is a case of keeping an Alehouse open before 11.30, or between 3 & 5pm on Christmas Day. Who was the sad sod that checked?

Charles Bower's gravestone

As landlord, Charles Bower left only one certain trace on the pub; a broken stone slab, currently set in the kitchen floor, inscribed 'Charles Bower. Licensed to Sell Tea & Snuff &c' explaining why, in 1867, he was described as a shopkeeper. The Tithe map of 1840 yields nothing on The Square, the site being 'Not Tithable', often reflecting the terms of tenure before the Dissolution of the Monasteries.

Bower died in August 1869, his broken headstone, almost illegible, leaning against the north wall of Langton church. Martha, along with her daughter, Mary, then 22, continued to hold the Inn. Mary married John Miller Hatchard, a Worth man, in 1873. A coincidence: he wasn't the John Miller who, by 1875, was landlord and remained so for more than ten years. William Hopkins was listed as landlord in 1889. By 1891, George Trent was in command, but the Grim Reaper left his widow, Mary, holding the reins as licensee in 1895 and then 1898.

Charles Bower, licensed to sell teas and snuff etc.

		William Turner	Son	Unm	[illegible]		Stonemason	[illegible]
		John Turner	Son	Unm	[illegible]		Horse & Car Proprietor	Wor[illegible]
	1	Jeramiah Bower	Head	Mar	[illegible]		Stoneminer	Wor[illegible]
		Elizabeth Bower	Wife	Mar		48		Wor[illegible]
		Walter Bower	Son	Unm	[illegible]		Stonemason	Wor[illegible]
		Eliza Ann Bower	Daur	Unm		21	Dressmaker	Wo[illegible]
	1	James Bridle	Head	Mar	[illegible]		Carpenter	Dorset Co[illegible]
		Mary A Bridle	Wife	Mar		64		St[illegible]
		Florance Bridle	Grand Daur			11	Scholar	Wa[illegible]
		Sarah Bower	Neice			14	do	Wor[illegible]
	1	Robert Day	Head	Mar	[illegible]		Fisherman	Swa[illegible]
		Elizabeth Day	Wife	Mar		32		Wor[illegible]
Square & Compass	1	John Miller	Head	Mar	[illegible]		Inn Keeper	Wor[illegible]
		Amellia Miller	Wife	Mar		28		Pimlico
		Annie M. Miller	Daur			7m		Worth
		Emily Bower	Servant			[illegible]	Scholar	Black[illegible]
Total of Houses...	4		Total of Males and Females...		11	13		

—*Draw the pen through such of the words of the headings as are inappropriate.* 1881 Worth Census. Wife born Pimlico Middx

PUBLIC RECORD OFFICE Reference:- RG 11/2098.

The Square and Compass landlord, John Miller, and family on 1881 Census

There is a cruel face to drinking. In October 1892, the NSPCC brought a case against Amos Bower of Langton. He was sentenced to six weeks hard labour for neglecting two sons, the eldest aged twelve. A widower, he spent his earnings at an unnamed public house, whilst the boys, filthy and starving, hovered outside. When their maternal grandmother remonstrated, Bower replied "Let them go to hell, where their * * * * mother is gone." Sometimes the boys went two days without eating and they were continually prowling around the village shop seeking for food.

The 20th century opened with Edwin Brixey at the helm. Born in Bourton in 1842, he moved to Wareham, marrying Annie Rendall in March 1870. In 1881, they were living in West Street with five children (only one a son) and his mother-in-law. He was a blacksmith, another tie between that industry and liquor! In 1901 and 1903 he ran The Square, but by 1907 Annie held the lease. From her it passed to Charles Newman.

No. 311.

ENGLAND.

PUBLICAN'S LICENCE. No. 342

6/73

SOUTHAMPTON Collection.

I, the undersigned, duly authorized by the Commissioners of Inland Revenue, hereby grant Licence to

of * Annie Brixey

to exercise and carry on the Trade or Business of a RETAILER of SPIRITS in a house situate at † and

in the Parish of Worth Matravers within the Administrative County ‡ of DORSET,

and known by the sign of Square & Compasses

and TO SELL BY RETAIL therein, SPIRITS, WINE, SWEETS, MADE WINES, MEAD, METHEGLIN, BEER, CIDER, and PERRY, to be consumed either on or off the premises, from the day of the date hereof, until and including the Tenth day of October next ensuing, such house, together with the offices, courts, yards and gardens therewith occupied, being of the annual value of £ 18 ; and I also hereby grant Licence to her to deal in and sell TOBACCO and SNUFF in the said house during the term above-mentioned, She having paid for this Licence, being § AN ORDINARY Licence, the undermentioned Duties, amounting to the Sum of £ 10 – 5 – 3

Dated this Eleventh day of October, 1906.

	£	s	d.
Retailer of Spirits	8	„	„
Dealer in Tobacco	-	5	3
Compensation Fund Charge, under Licensing Act, 1904	2	„	„
Total ......£	10	„ 5	„ 3

Thos. J. Buck

Collector of Inland Revenue.

INLAND REVENUE OFFICE

G & S 5027 [4339] 20 bks. 1/06 (465) [OVER.

Annie Brixey's licence

WILLIAM NEWMAN

WILLIAM NEWMAN
m. 14 February, 1802, Sturminster Newton
ANN NEWMAN

EDWARD NEWMAN *b.c. 15 July, 1802*
m. 2 July, 1829, Sturminster Newton
ELIZABETH UPSHALL *b.c. 1810*

JAMES	SELINA	JAMES	EMILY	GEORGE & HENRY	DELINA	RUBIN	ELLEN	CHARLES
c.	*c.*	*c.*	*c.*	*c.*	*b.c.*	*c.*	*c.*	*c.*
21 December, 1830	*6 January, 1833*	*7 February, 1836*	*8 May, 1838*	*9 May, 1840*	*1841*	*16 December,1843*	*20 December,1845*	*4 April, 1849*
		m.						
		23 October, 1858						
		JOHANNA NORTHOVER						

EDWARD	WILLIAM	SELINA	LOUISA	SAMUEL	HENRY	WALTER (SYDNEY)	CHARLES	GEORGE	'M'
c.	*c.*	*c.*	*b.c.*	*c.*	*b.c.*	*b.c.*	*b.c.*	*b.c.*	*b.c.*
4 March, 1859	*11 October, 1860*	*10 May, 1863*	*1864*	*2 April, 1865*	*1868*	*1871*	*1872*	*1872*	*1873*
					c.	*c.*	*c.*	*c.*	
					6 April, 1873	*6 April, 1873*	*6 April, 1873*	*6 April, 1873*	
							m.		
							16 April, 1906		
							FLORENCE LEGG		
							b.c.		
							1883		

CHARLES	EILEEN
b.c. June 1906 m.	*b.*
FRANCES BURT	*6 January, 1911*
b. 9 June, 1903	

RAYMOND
b. 23 February, 1931
m. 8 December, 1956
STELLA SMITH
b. 26 June, 1931

MARY	CHARLIE
b. 26 September, 1960	*b. 20 March, 1966*

The known Newman family tree

The Newmans enter

Charles Newman was born at Goff's Corner, Sturminster Newton in 1871, his father, James, being a farm labourer. Parish records list a fair number of Newmans in Sturminster Newton. Two appear on the First World War memorial but the modern phone book lists only one. The family was well established in the town by the 18th century.

Beer is in the blood: two Newmans, James and William, held alehouses in Sutrminster Newton in 1738. James offered surety for a license application in nearby Okeford Fitzpaine, before disappearing from the alehouse registers (A James Newman amongst burials for 1740 probably accounts for his disappearance). William featured until 1753, when his alehouse is named as The Whitehart. In 1754 a William Newman was buried and Robert Newman put up surety for three license applications. In 1759, when Sturminster Newton's alehouses were listed again, there was no Newman landlord, nor any Whitehart. Robert Newman, yeoman, offered surety for the landlord of The Red Lion in 1769. Beyond that, the registers were destroyed. Later, a Charles Newman creeps in; between 1823 and 1828 he is holding The Crown in Sturminster. In 1830, Elizabeth Newman, presumably his widow, is licensee before it passes out of Newman hands.

James, William and Charles were almost certainly related to our Charles Newman, since he descended from two Newman lines by the marriage of William Newman to Ann Newman in 1802. In 1801 a census in Sturminster Newton listed four Newman households. An Ann born to William and Charity Newman in 1782 was not with them in 1801. Was she married, in service or dead? Another Ann, born in 1788 to Samuel and Elizabeth, could have married William at fourteen. Perhaps his Ann came from elsewhere. In 1801, William and Charity Newman of house 144 have an unmarried, yet working, William in their household. If he was their son, he was 26 or less in 1802.

In 1801, all four Newman households were employed in the textile industry. There was a huge appetite for cloth at the time, and weavers flourished. Lancashire weavers could earn six times the wage of a farm labourer. The boom, due to increased output of machine-spun yarn, doesn't explain these Newmans. Although all the men, save one, were weavers, their women were spinning by hand. Was textile work a

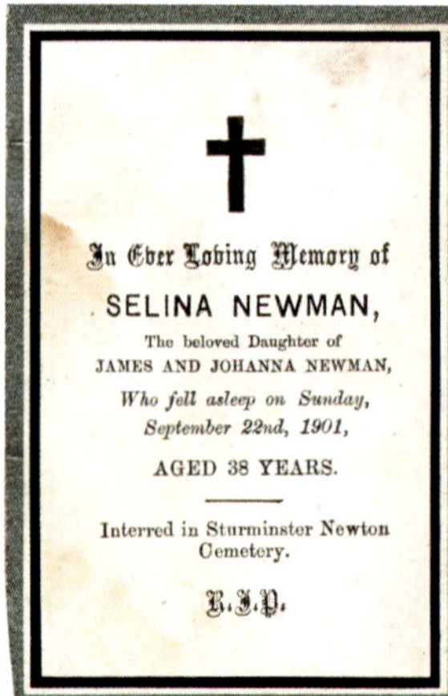

In Ever Loving Memory of
SELINA NEWMAN,
The beloved Daughter of
JAMES AND JOHANNA NEWMAN,
Who fell asleep on Sunday,
September 22nd, 1901,
AGED 38 YEARS.

Interred in Sturminster Newton Cemetery.

R.I.P.

The early loss of Selina Newman and, right, possible family from Sturminster Newton

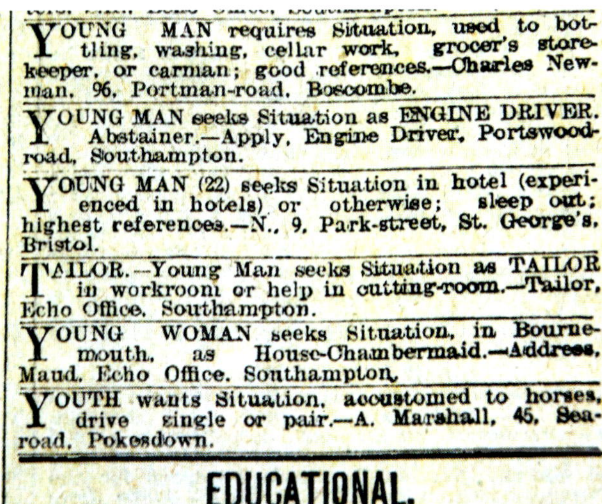

YOUNG MAN requires Situation, used to bottling, washing, cellar work, grocer's storekeeper, or carman; good references.—Charles Newman, 96, Portman-road, Boscombe.

YOUNG MAN seeks Situation as ENGINE DRIVER. Abstainer.—Apply, Engine Driver, Portswood-road, Southampton.

YOUNG MAN (22) seeks Situation in hotel (experienced in hotels) or otherwise; sleep out; highest references.—N., 9, Park-street, St. George's, Bristol.

TAILOR.—Young Man seeks Situation as TAILOR in workroom or help in cutting-room.—Tailor, Echo Office, Southampton.

YOUNG WOMAN seeks Situation, in Bournemouth, as House-Chambermaid.—Address, Maud, Echo Office, Southampton.

YOUTH wants Situation, accustomed to horses, drive single or pair.—A. Marshall, 45, Sea-road, Pokesdown.

EDUCATIONAL.

Charlie's advert in the Bournemouth Echo

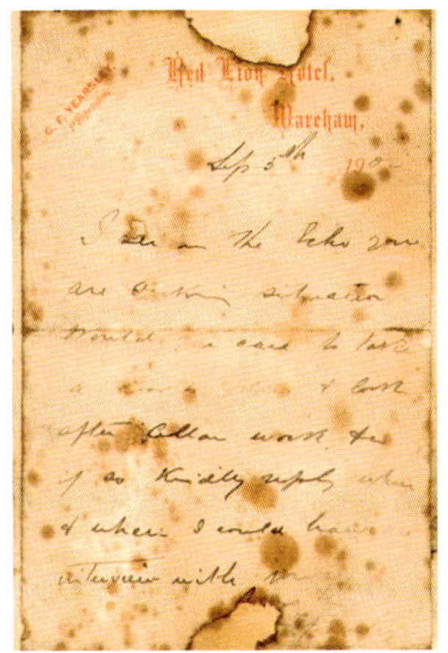

Red Lion Hotel,
Wareham.

Mr Yearsley offers an interview at The Red Lion, Wareham

family tradition? Suddenly, in the 1820s, the introduction of power-weaving brought catastrophic unemployment. James, born in 1836, became a farm labourer.

Charlie's habit of writing notes on the fly-leaves of books fills in several details of his life. In 1891, he lived in Christchurch, helping to build Bournemouth's Metropole Hotel. In 1901 he was at home in Sturminster Newton. He reached Worth via Wareham. In a 'situations wanted' advertisement in the Daily Echo of 2nd September 1902, Charlie, already 31 and giving a Boscombe address, listed 'cellar work' or 'car man' as possible employments. Mr Yearsley, proprietor of 'The Red Lion Hotel, Wareham' replied, asking if he would be interested in cellar work.

In a sentence added to a report in the weekly, The Poole and Dorset Herald, dated Sept 4th 1902, a Mr & Mrs G. B. Newman of Springbourne acknowledged condolences. Their son, Cecil, had drowned on the 18th August while swimming off Boscombe Pier. So, in the same week, G. and Charles Newman, both connected with then-small Boscombe, featured in newspapers. Was 'G. Newman' related to Charlie, or was it merely a coincidence?

Yearsley gave Charlie the job. He spent five years working at The Red Lion where, a century earlier, The Sloop had been auctioned. He was ambitious and, when Brixey died, probably heard through The Red Lion (also a Strong pub) that Annie planned

to quit. In 1907, he had enough capital to apply for the lease of The Square and Compass. Strong probably preferred a tenant the company already knew.

Perhaps there was little competition. What was Worth Matravers in the 1900s? A small, isolated village on no important route, populated by stone cutters, farm workers and a few fishermen. There was little hope of making a fortune there. But fortune is fickle.

Annie Brixey employed a valuer to price any pub furnishings Charlie required. The Brixeys probably inherited most of them, her husband having made a similar arrangement with his predecessor. The list comprised deal tables, stools and benches, some still in use. Six spittoons have gone the way of all spittoons. She even listed a small piece of linoleum. Most numerous among the beer and spirit glasses were the forty-one ware quart cups, a quart being quarter of a gallon. There were metal and glass spirit measures, taps, hammers, funnels and cans for the beer, even wire netting to cover the fowl run. So there were chickens in her day.

There were indoor games, too, including a circular board with hooks and rings, presumably for throwing rings onto the hooks, a sport later replaced by darts. There was a bagatelle board. Bagatelle, created for a royal party at Chateau de Bagatelle, was the pinball of its day, played with a cue. The object was to avoid pins on the board while sinking nine balls into numbered holes. No shove ha'penny board, large or small, appeared on the inventory.

The house comprised three licensed rooms, a cellar, a living room (now the museum), pantry and scullery. Upstairs were four bedrooms, outside, a fuel house, two pigsties constructed of stone slates, a two-stall stable and trap house (for the pony and trap). An 'E.C.' disguises an earth closet. Water came from a well, a wellhead remaining at the east end of the building. Presumably, the pump that stood near the back door was one of Charlie's innovations.

Annie renewed her license in October 1906; Charlie bought the remaining time. His rent, £16 quarterly, started from 8th March 1907. The accompanying land measured 33 perches, priced at £2 per perch. (1 perch = 25 sq m) The structures were valued at £464. Repairs were in the hands of the brewer, but inside labour was left to the tenant. That explains why, seventy years later, when Raymond wanted a new stand for his barrels, Whitbread paid for the timber but Ray arranged for Keith Lovell to do the work.

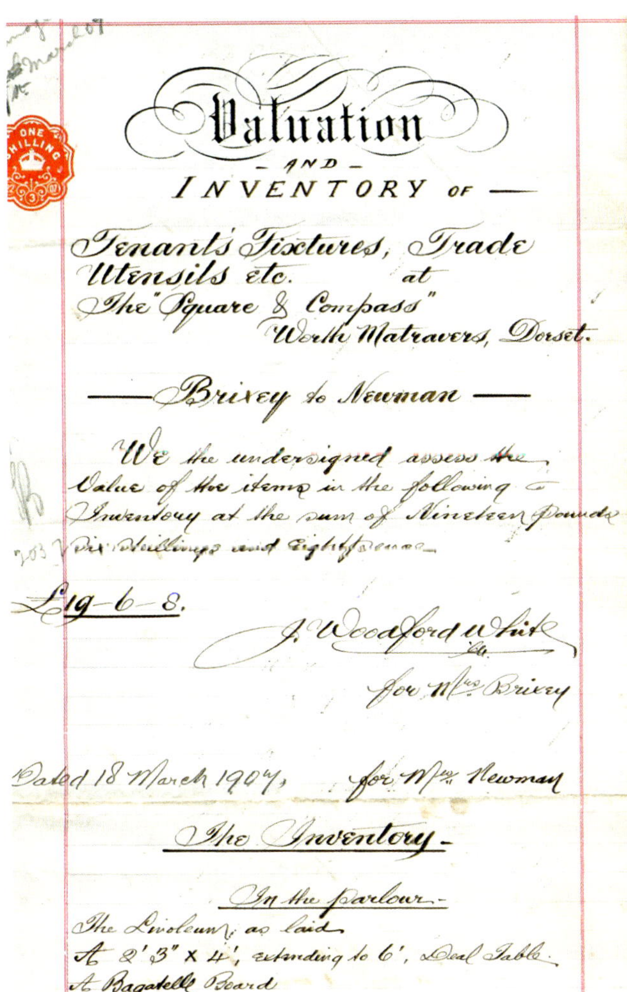

Valuation
and
INVENTORY of —
Tenant's Fixtures, Trade
Utensils etc. at
The "Square & Compass"
Worth Matravers, Dorset.

— Brixey to Newman —

We the undersigned assess the Value of the items in the following Inventory at the sum of Nineteen Pounds Six Shillings and Eightpence

£19–6–8.

J. Woodford White
for Mrs Brixey

Dated 18 March 1907, for Mr Newman

The Inventory –

In the parlour –

The Linoleum, as laid
A 2' 3" x 4', extending to 6', Deal Table
A Bagatelle Board

Inventory transferring lock-stock-and-barrel to Charlie Newman on the 18th March, 1907 and marking the start of the Newman century

CAUTION.

THE COMMISSIONERS OF INLAND REVENUE hereby give notice that the Revenue Laws impose penalties in respect of the Adulteration of the goods specified below, or the sale of any such goods Adulterated, and that such Laws will be strictly enforced.

BEER.

1. A DEALER IN, OR RETAILER OF BEER may not adulterate or dilute Beer, or add any matter or thing thereto (except finings for the purpose of clarification).

2. A DEALER IN, OR RETAILER OF BEER may not receive or have in his custody or possession any sugar, saccharine substance, extract, or syrup (except for domestic use, the proof whereof shall lie on him), or any preparation for increasing the gravity of Beer.

TOBACCO AND SNUFF.

3. NO PERSON may prepare, or have in possession, any material in imitation of, or to be mixed with, Tobacco or Snuff, or deliver to any Manufacturer of Tobacco, any such material.

4. A MANUFACTURER, DEALER, OR RETAILER may not receive, have in possession, or send out any Tobacco or Snuff to which has been added any other article than is permitted by law to be used in the manufacture of the same (except Cavendish or Negro-head, under the aftermentioned regulations), or any Snuff which, after being dried at 212°F., is found to contain more than 26 per cent. of the carbonates, chlorides, and sulphates of potassium, sodium, and ammonium, inclusive of the salts of potassium, sodium, and ammonium naturally present in the Tobacco; and in the case of Welsh and Irish Snuff, the same must not contain more than 13 per cent. of the oxides of calcium and magnesium, including the lime derived from the lime water which may be legally added thereto.

5. A DEALER IN, OR RETAILER of Tobacco may not have in his possession any Tobacco containing a greater proportion of oil than 1 per cent., or which, on being dried at 212°F., is found to decrease in weight more than 32 per cent.

6. CAVENDISH OR NEGRO-HEAD containing sweetening or flavouring matters, made in bond or imported, may only be kept and sold, provided it is contained in packets secured by a proper Customs label. Each packet must be sold entire and the label obliterated or spoiled by the seller at the time of delivering such packet to a purchaser.

I hereby transfer my rights & interest in this licence to Charles Newman
Signed Annie Brixey
March 8th 1907.
Witness J. Woodford White
Valuer

Transferred according to Charles Newman
Entry 23/3/07

Annie Brixey's 1906 licence is signed over to Charlie Newman

The glorious reign of Charles the First: The beginning (1907–18)

CN establishing tablet

Charles Newman arrived at The Square in March 1907, having married Florence Legg of Puddletown the previous April, at the unusually late age of 36. Just in time, it seems, because their son, Charles, was born the same year. Young Charlie has a book inscribed to Florence, a prize for attending Woodsford Church Sunday School 350 times out of 416 in the year 1894-95. Marriage fitted well with Charlie's aspirations; a good woman was essential for running a pub.

Charlie must have seen The Square as a step towards better things. Three factors made it more: his character, Florence's abilities and Fashion. Charlie, an intelligent, amusing extrovert, was ideally suited to charm another class of clientele whilst retaining the locals. Florence's food drew praise. At the turn of the century, the Bloomsbury set favoured nearby Studland. After WW I, as plans for a chain ferry threatened Studland's exclusivity, a new artistic wave turned to other parts of Purbeck. Some reached Worth.

Charlie and wife Florence

The Square at the beginning of the last century

When the Newmans moved in, The Square looked much as it does now. There were more panes in some of the windows, solid wooden shutters protected them during gales. Notices announcing the pub's name were differently distributed and there was no picture on the main sign. Only at the east end is major change apparent. A lean-to stood against the east wall. The stable, later a garage and finally a store, was detached from the rest of the building, projecting beyond the façade line and opening westwards, towards the modern museum wing.

Did the Newmans arrive with a pony and trap? A photograph of the façade around 1912 shows one; it would have been essential for operating an isolated inn. First World War photographs show a sign, 'Pony and Trap for Hire', above the stable door. Now, only wreckage survives from a couple of horse-drawn vehicles. Other early photographs indicate that the projecting museum wing held a 'Tea & Coffee Room'. There was also a small 'Square and Compass' logo beneath a sign advertising Strong & Co.

What happened during those first Newman years? Had Mrs Brixey taken guests? She may have put up the occasional tired walker, but perhaps The Square only started to exploit trippers in 1913. That Spring, Charlie opened a Visitors' Book, and his

Charlie James aged 2 ½, 1909

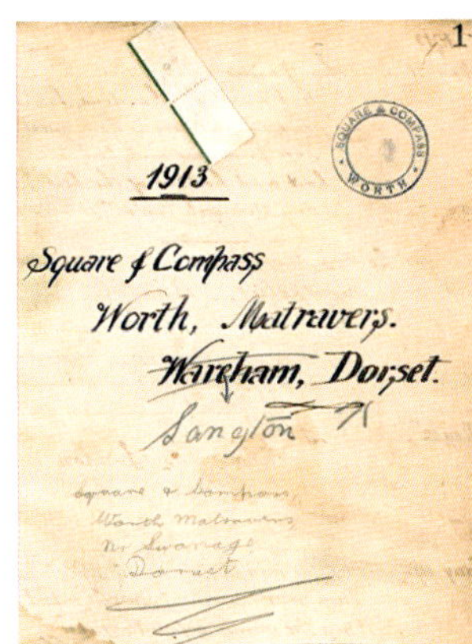

1

1913

Square & Compass

Worth, Matravers.

Wareham, Dorset.

1913 Visitors' Book, page 1

Charlie Newman and son

first guest, on May 11th, along with one John James Jarvis, was his favourite brother, George, who was settled in Bristol. Jarvis writes "If peace and quietness is your quest/ Free from care and toil / A host and hostess of the best / Say stranger, you've 'struck oil'." To which George adds "To be a poet, I cannot aspire / but pray allow me to say / The words expressed a few lines higher / Echo my thoughts if I may."
Were they friends, arriving together? The brothers remained close throughout life. When George died in 1949, although he was buried in Bristol, Charlie raised an inscription to him in Worth churchyard.

Those were inauspicious times. The madness of 1914 loomed, a marvellous summer descending into four years of the worst slaughter Europe has ever seen. Proportionately, WW I took its greatest toll from the upper echelons, the sons of those who had failed to prevent it. Many of those young Lieutenants and Captains who wrote in the Visitor's Book were fated to end torn meat, throttled in French mud.

Florence Newman with soldiers from the Dorsetshire Regiment

The first breath of war invades the book on August 13th 1914: "M.E Peau-Brockley – Ella, Nellie, Mary, Marion/ Refugees from Dinard, France. Vive l'Angleterre et Vive la France." There is the scent of the easily-led. A note of sedition emerges the following month with J. F. Franklin's verse: "All men here are born alike / In this and every nation / The rich among the poor would be / But for wealth and education / But when we are all laid in our graves / With a hundred years to back it / Who'll know whose bones are they / That wear a xxxxx (Illegible – why not 'scarlet jacket'?)"

From January 1915, soldiers appear in the pages. There was a large army encampment north of Swanage, at Ballard Estate (which originally consisted of army huts) and Ulwell. Some regiments named frequently in the Visitors' Book, such as the 13th Battalion of Royal Warwickshire Regt, were probably stationed there. The first men to sign the book at the end of January weren't that lucky. They belonged to the 9th Hants Battalion the 9th (Cyclist) Battalion of the Royal Hampshire Regiment – which was made up of motorcyclists. Apparently, their mission was to protect the coast. Cyclist P.C. Diamond 'known to Scotland Yard as Dido' left a couple of lines: 'Chatman's Pool is none too cool in the summer time, / But in November and December its enough to kill mankind.' Cyclist C.H.Dance, 'The 9th Hants Battn Poet' gave more: '2 Sentrys stand up side by side / At a place called Chapmans Pool…' but there is a happy ending. They were billeted at The Square, with good old Hampshire BEER (Strong of Romsey, remember) and Mrs Newman's delicious sausages. Two days later, without regrets, Cyclist T. Thorne 'The Battalion Prickle', more gifted than his fellows, wrote: 'Tideless Pool is beautiful / Is the mud still there / Do the rats still run around the windless / In Portland's glare / You slip and slide so easily / Is your rifle all right / What would I give to be with them / In the old boathouse to night.'

Cyclist Battalion badge

Soldiers on the move

Sergeant Jacobs described himself as 'One of the Hero Motor-cyclists now protecting this charming little pub!' Two Despatch Riders in RE Signals turned up. A bandsman, C. Fitzgerald, complained of his duty: 'at peveril point we stand and freeze / listening to the roaring seas /…' but he warned '…this song is strictly prohibited to be sung in a tap room by Order of the Boot.' So these boys add a snippet of historical knowledge to their banter: the tap room is the place to drink in 1915, not a kitchen or larder.

What did Private W. Monk from Victoria Docks, London make of his visit to the country? Having set a wild scene, probably at Chapmans Pool, he started a second

Charlie James…
…and grandmother

verse with 'Here two sentries age eighteen' were detailed for a nasty night watch. It came to an end and, after breakfast and a wash 'Then to the tap room we proceed / And playing rings one takes the lead…' Is that the 'board and rings' Mrs Brixey passed on to Charlie? But they are lucky as 'Sentries in Billets at The Square and Compass.' If he survived the holocaust, did France drive from him all memory of these gentler beginnings, the guard duties in friendly night?

W. Ingram of Blandford, another young sentry, composed a similar long poem, then added a second in a very different mould. This kid had yet to see the mud, the filth, the uselessness when he wrote 'Hark my lads the bugle calls / We care not for those German foes / We English lads are hard as steel. / We care not for old Kaiser Bill'… Ingram is not listed amongst Dorset's dead. He left the field an older and wiser man.

That June, M. Dewell, from Canada, storekeeper on the SS Tortona, signed. What brought him, he doesn't say. Apart from the cyclists, the soldiers who wrote were mostly officers – lieutenants and second lieutenants – the educated cream of

their era. The 13th Royal Warwicks came first, with 2nd Lieut Phillips and Capt Tullidge, perhaps young guys not long out of school, joining up for adventure, pressurised by propaganda which made Germany the current Empire of Evil.

The Warwicks, dominating until late October, were replaced by several disparate groups. The RFA (Royal Field Artillery) emerge as prominent. In November, four young officers begin: "Mann ist was er ist' the Huns exclaim…' – since this means 'man is what he is' they had a good, fatalistic point. Whatever their philosophy, they were back the following month. What was Pfc C A Kazmierczak, CO 'C' 705 T D Bn, Grafton, Ohio doing here in May 1916? The Americans didn't enter the war until 1917.

H Carr, giving no rank, only 2 5 Devons, contributed "When this you see / Remember me / Tho' many miles we distant be."

After May 1916 the groups of soldiers, probably representing those encamped nearby, stopped coming. There are only two individual soldiers for the rest of the war. Lieut A. H. Haysom of the RAFC, in July, adds his name so very faintly in pencil; a local man? In June 1917, was Sergeant Whitby No 15 (Artists) OCB the vanguard of a coming invasion?

Eileen arrives

A couple, the Denyers, turn up twice, giving the address as Park Hospital, Lewisham. One comments 'Mrs Newman is one of the nicest women I've ever seen'. What was the hospital? Was he war wounded, shell shocked, along with his wife, mother, brother? Did the landlady, ignoring his injuries, treat him kindly? So easy to read what is not there.

On a beautiful April day in 1916 a woman, no name, merely initials, became the most poignant wartime visitor: 'When I arrived at Worth at 3,/ And found no service there would be,/ I then began to want some tea; / But first I thought the church I'd see, / So had a welcome rest there free. / My soldier lad – ah! Would that he / Had been this lovely day with me. A lonely woman, NH.' I hope he came back to her.

Throughout the carnage, people came, leaving cheerful little poems or sketches, ignoring the guns across the Channel. They, too, lived in the shadow of the slaughter; no one was isolated from those guns. When three school boys arrived in October 1916, one name, P. C. Boileau, caught my eye. A.H. E. Boileau crossed my part of India in 1831, keeping an interesting journal, sketching familiar places and writing execrable poetry. This boy's passing was marked by 'good butter, better than school.' A few years older and he, too, could have added a rosy tint to Flanders mud.

George 'Buff' Bower

Another child intruded on those serious times, and she was here to stay. Crossing a 1916 page in large, ill-formed letters is EILEEN MAY NEWMAN, born that year, but perhaps scrawling six years later, when the book remerged. It is struck out. She was probably spanked; life did not treat Eileen generously.

Local men who drank at the pub were gathered up into that dreadful war. Amongst Old Charlie's photographs is a large one, enhanced and sharpened, of a sturdy, youthful private soldier. The care with which the picture has been retouched suggests the only image of one who fell for King and Country. On it is written 'Private George Bower, The Lane, Worth Matravers'. Like most local Bowers, a nickname differentiates him from all others: he was 'Buff' Bower, one of the survivors, well-known amongst the quarrying fraternity. An added note says 'Later known as 'Buff' when his moustache grew stronger! Short for Buffalo of course.' Knowing of 'Buff' since my teens, I never knew, till now, the origin of the name.

Eileen and family, and the page she defaced

47

Mar 23/1916 J. MacGregor Knox. RFA

" " R Smith. RFA.

~~Eileen May~~

This Inn is "it"

"some" Inn. M.B.

and so is the Landlord M.B.

& so say all of us.

The shadow of war – years of fame – Old Charlie (1918–30)

Something happened at the close of 1917 to remove the Visitors' Book from circulation. Did the death of someone close to Charlie take a toll on his spirit, or was it the very mass of dead? Or were there banal reasons – the book mislaid, to turn up again in 1921? Those missing years saw dark depression as the survivors took stock.

More death was to come. On 9th January 1920, the SS Treveal, returning from Calcutta with a cargo of jute, hit Kimmeridge Ledges in rough weather. Next morning, the captain, fearing the ship was breaking up, abandoned ship and made for Chapmans Pool. Of 43 men, seven survived. Charlie, helping to identify the dead, found a postcard in one man's pocket – from his children looking forward to his return. The dead were laid out in Worth's reading room – now the tea-room – but for half a dozen put in The Square's Parlour. In The Square, on Monday 12th January, Mr Maddock, Deputy Coroner for East Dorset, held an inquest on 20 of the crew. The jury suggested that 'telephonic communication' be established between Worth and the coastguard station at St Aldhelms Head. Soon The Square had Worth's only telephone.

Charlie provided transport. The first time Peggy Odam (later Paterson) came, in 1920, '...Charley Newman drove us up Kingston Hill in his wagonette'. She wasn't the only one. A bill for ten shillings survives, dated August 1st 1921, for transporting Worth Band to Swanage. Either the band was small or Charlie's vehicle large! He was prospering. At the Worth sales of 1919 and 1923, he bought land on which he built White Lodge, Compass Cottage and Channel View (the site of Young Charlie's new house). He also built Braemar, opposite the church, for his son, adding a stone inscribed 'CN to CN', which his son, irritated, rendered over. It reappeared when the house was being demolished.

In 1920, Charles Rennie Mackintosh, the pioneering architect, and his wife stayed with Francis Newbery in Corfe. Newbery, when principal of Glasgow School of Art, had taught Mackintosh to paint; the school's new building was designed by Mackintosh. Newbery, of Bridport origin, retired to Corfe with his wife, beaten down by deep depression, having seen his best pupils slain. The evidence that they

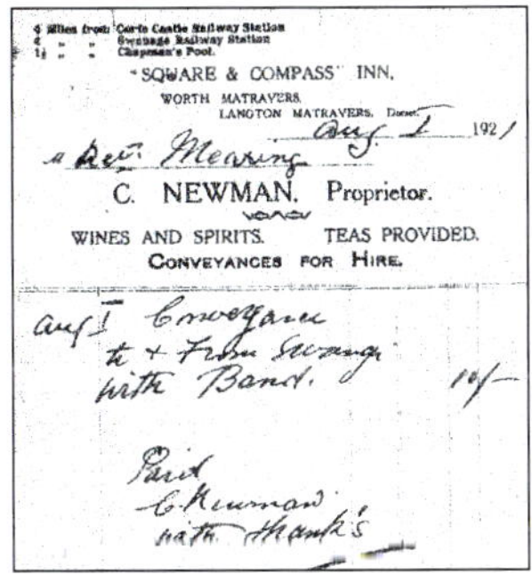

4 Miles from Corfe Castle Railway Station
4 " " Swanage Railway Station
1½ " " Chapman's Pool.

"SQUARE & COMPASS" INN,
WORTH MATRAVERS,
LANGTON MATRAVERS, Dorset. Aug 1 1921

C. NEWMAN, Proprietor.

WINES AND SPIRITS. TEAS PROVIDED.
CONVEYANCES FOR HIRE.

Aug 1 Conveyance to + From Swanage with Band. 10/–

Paid C. Newman with thank's

Worth Band conveyance bill

Channel View and White Lodge

Braemar

CN stone

Mackintosh at Worth Matravers

by Jo Draper

Rennie Mackintosh's paintings

visited The Square? Quite simply, Mackintosh's stylised painting of Worth, inspired by the view from the pub. The Newberys probably took him there because it was a favourite outing. Francis ('Fra') left his mark, creating the war memorial gateway to Corfe cemetery, the town sign and the paintings above and behind the altar of Swanage's Catholic Church, which overlooked me as an altar-boy. Perhaps the photographers, Joan and Helen Muspratt, came up to The Square with him. Certainly, Joan, who never struck me as a woman to go pubbing on her own, took photographs of the building.

By 11th September 1921, poets were back in the visitors' book. E Powys Mathers and R. C. Mathers contributed a piece that, quite uncharacteristically, bridged the divide between two communities, the educated outsiders and the local working men. The Mathers, of the former group, mentioned Hooper and Mrs Hooper, Billie Bower of Winspit (Billy Winspit's first entry into Square history) and a Mr Green in their record of a very drunken night, or was it day? It all turns on PM and AM. "...It was here Miss Greenslade grew, man / Amorous of me and you, man / Gave them tea at half past two, man... / Here's to all of us, Charlie Newman." The Hoopers, stationed at the coastguard cottages on St Aldhelms Head, completed their three year stint in February 1923. It is there in the book!

Edward Powys Mathers, then 29, was a poet and orientalist. His version of The Book of a Thousand and One Nights came out two years later, but he had already translated a Kashmiri poet, Bilhana, and 120 Asian love poems under the title 'The Garden of Bright Waters'. Aaron Copeland set some of his work to music. Under the alias 'Torquemada', he created cryptic crossword puzzles for The Observer! At least, that is one story. Graham Greene states equally firmly that two of his teachers, the improbably-named Mr Hill and Mr Dale, together created the 'Torquemada' crosswords.

Agnes Hoare, a wartime visitor, returned in June 1922 and there is a drawing of the pub with a sign in front reading 'Strong & Co Bass Teas'. Florence Newman's cream teas earned much praise, as did her blackcurrant jam. At tea-time, The Square showed a different face, the bibulous replaced by the respectable. Families stopped to recover after walking to the Head or spending a day at Winspit or Chapman's Pool. The alcohol drinkers were more poetically fertile, occasionally referring to the pub as 'The Bank'. Early maps didn't use the definite article, just 'Bank'.

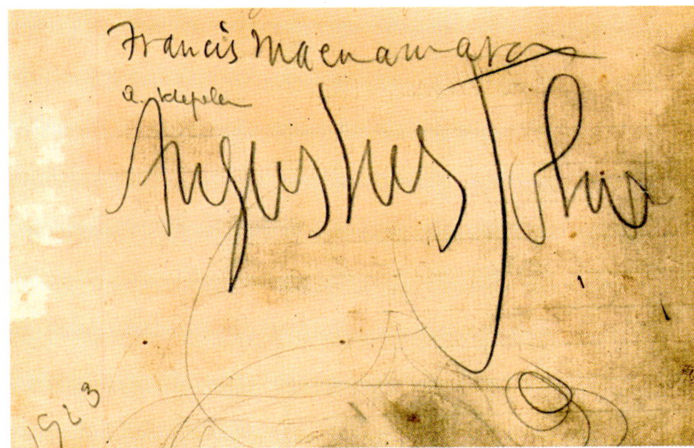

John's signature with his sketch of Charlie

One large signature on 8th August 1923 has pushed all others aside in the pub's roll of fame. Augustus John signed alongside Francis Macnamara and another, difficult signature, which Jack suggests was A. Schepeler. Alex Schepeler, settled in London but born in Minsk, at twenty became one of John's models in 1909 but soon disappeared from his biography. Did she take a break from a fifty year career as secretary at Illustrated London News to visit The Square?

A month after he signed, John met Thomas Hardy and embarked on a portrait, of which Hardy said "I don't know if that is how I look, but that is how I feel.". (He also said "If I look like that, the sooner I am under the ground the better.") Were diversions to The Square ever related to trips to Hardy's Dorchester home? John bought a cottage in Fordingbridge in 1927 and came to Worth regularly, spending several days drinking with Old Charlie until, utterly inebriated, he returned home to paint. Rhoda Bower, Billy Winspit's widow, reckons he continued to come after WW II.

John, one of Britain's leading early 20th century painters, was notable for his free love and ever-expanding family. His sister, Gwen, sometime mistress of Auguste Rodin, was also a fine painter, but she lived mostly in France. Although both Johns came to Swanage in 1909, there is no evidence that Gwen ever darkened The Square's door. Augustus left a sketch of Charlie, drawn in 1924 on a numbered page from the Visitors' Book, which explains the absence of page 100. It is now over the mantlepiece of the Big Room. Charlie saved a 1952 cutting showing Augustus John at his daughter's wedding.

THE DAILY MAIL, THURSDAY, MARCH 6, 1952

Augustus John's Daughter Weds

Article on John kept by Charlie

Low's portrait of Augustus John

What of MacNamara? An Irish writer, he fits neatly into a group of young poets and artists settled in London who indulged in a Bohemian lifestyle in the wild shadow of the war. They questioned the crabbed values of the good and worthy who had consigned their peers to the carnage. His daughter was to marry Dylan Thomas and rumour places Thomas, too, at The Square. They say he slept in the porch. MacNamara married again to John's sister-in-law then, with a third wife, turned his family home in Ireland into a successful hotel.

The no-less-famous New Zealander, David Low, came, too. Born in 1891, he was inspired by English comics and was only eleven when his first strip appeared. He settled in England in 1919 and, as 'Low', drew newspaper cartoons, especially for The Evening Standard, The Daily Herald and The Manchester Guardian. He created Colonel Blimp, the archetypal voice of British reaction. Cartoons of Hitler and Mussolini put him on the Gestapo's black list. Less disreputable than John, he died in 1963 as Sir David Low. His contribution to The Square is a pencil drawing of Augustus John, also above the Big Room's fireplace.

Occasionally, the visitors' book contains variably accomplished drawings of the pub or its view. Leslie Moffat Ward, a well known local artist, left a good sketch down the valley towards Chapmans Pool and Portland and a print in the Big Room of Swanage's Mill Pond. He signs next to William Waddington of Windemere and

Leslie Moffat Ward sketch of Hill Bottom towards Portland

Leslie Moffat Ward print of The Millpond from the Big Room

S. H. Braithwaite, both linked to the Lakeside Artists. Some sketches help to place alterations to the building. One, from 1916, shows the stable block still separate from the body of the building. Another, from 1927, shows them joined, as they are today.

A new game features in several entries for 1923. Rex Buvery had 'jolly good ninepins' and Archibald Russell 'Lost Game of Skittles, fine Tea.', but they are talking of the same thing. Russell was Lancaster Herald in the College of Arms in the 1930s, where his portrait still hangs. He built a handsome retirement home in Swanage, and was for many years President of the Dorset Natural History and Archaeological Society. The couple never recovered from losing both sons in WW II.

On the page before that John so cavalierly tore out two composers, Peter Warlock and E. J. Moeran, signed in July 1924. With them were A.E. & Rona Buckland, Percy and Alice Tower and A. or E. Burden, probably all connected with the English Singers, who played a major role in reviving early English songs, particularly Elizabethan madrigals. Warlock, whose real name was Philip Heseltine, was then thirty. His music, influenced by Tudor work, Celtic culture and Delius, received recognition after WW I, 'Corpus Christi' being a lament for the war dead. He corresponded with Augustus John during the 1920s, so their simultaneous entries were probably no coincidence.

Peter Warlock and E.J. Moeran's signatures

Both Warlock and Moeran wrote for the English singers, who would take a cottage at Ower for their practice sessions. The Towers came back to The Square at other times, sometimes with a couple called Tautz, who also appeared during WW I, and one Kathleen Hassan. Two other English Singers, a pioneering 'item', Ivor Notley and David Brynley settled at Little Woolgarston, in a cottage found for them by Hilda Spencer Watson. Although they must have visited The Square – they were that sort of folk – neither signs the book.

Portrait by unknown artist

As a critic, Warlock used his real name. (He chose a third one when editing an anthology on drinking: Rab Noolas. Try it backwards!) An eccentric character, another member of the 'London Boheme...' of... 'Painters, musicians, writers – hangers-on, models, advanced young people, anybody who is at outs with the conventions, and belongs nowhere in particular.' That is D.H. Lawrence writing in 1916, in 'Women in Love', where he satirised Heseltine as 'Julius Halliday'. Lawrence's depiction of 'a swarthy, slender young man with rather long, solid black hair hanging from under his black hat... a smile at once naïve and warm, and vapid'

of '…a high squealing voice' and '…an almost imbecile smile flickering palely on his face' was clearly familiar to a section of his readers. It inspired him to the error of litigation. It is no small achievement on Heseltine's part that, at only 22, he earned this assault from Lawrence. Three other novelists, including Aldous Huxley, parodied him. After putting out his cat, he gassed himself in 1930.

Ernest John Moeran, contemporary with Warlock, studied under Stanford at the Royal College of Music. He received a head wound in WW I, which plagued him with mental problems. He and Warlock lived together in Eynsford, Kent for several years during the 1920s and were notorious for their drunken excesses. The English Singers inspired him to write his idyll, 'Whythorne's Shadow' in 1931.

Frank Idle and his family, who visited in 1924, drew a cartoon of a black cat and the first line of a song, 'Felix kept on walking…' My mother used to sing it. "…By a train at Dover / Nearly got run over / Up into the air he flew / Landed very near Peru / And kept on walking still." I bet the words are wrong – she was generous with her interpretations. Idle would have known; he was an organ composer living in Bournemouth.

1926 saw the National Strike, when a short-lived periodical, 'Lansbury's Weekly', came to prominence. One of its staff, known simply as 'B', was in The Square that Boxing Day. There is a poem 'There was a young girl named Eileen / Who to Weymouth by bus had just been / She came back rather late / And said 'At fust Wor' gat / Drop I if you know what I mean.' Funny for the writer and his mates. How did ten-year-old Eileen feel?

Lionel Jellinek, who became one of Old Charlie's close circle, entered the book in 1926, aged 28. His verse praises 'Gold Label Scotch Whiskey'. Later, Lionel and Lydia Jellinek had a cottage at the entrance to Worth House and two children, Ann and an adopted Russian son. As a judge, Lionel used to bring his briefs down, working

Composer Frank Idle's signature with the first line of a song

on the train. In order to 'bag' an empty compartment – in an era when there were separate compartments throughout – he collected the tough discs of tissue that seal winkle shells and stuck them over his face like horrid scabs. No one dared join him. Lionel played the viola, whilst Kate Lawrence made and played violins. Together with Miss Stock, the music teacher from Langton and Floss Welsh (of the other Worth shop, Hooper and Welsh), who played the harmonium, they gave concerts in the church. Judge Jellinek continued to frequent the area and its music into the 1960s. One evening, at Mervyn Vicars' house in Swanage, he announced as he arrived, "I've just had a terrible week! Had to send a wretch down for buggery… now let's play some music."

Brother George Newman and Eileen

The twenties contributed most famous signatories to the book. Suddenly the place was fashionable and Charlie was not slow cashing in. The people who wrote or drew entries for him give only a taste of the spirit of the times. Many came repeatedly but only signed once. Many, no less famous, escaped without signing. Ordinary families and couples dropped by, holidaymakers quitting work in favour of the seaside. It is never clear which signatories stayed the night and which merely stopped for tea or a drink.

Some visitors were talented, whatever their artistic aspirations. There is a good little cartoon by one of five girls (labelled as P. Stagg, C. Hudson, E Watts, C Bradley (?) and B Johnson) with an accompanying verse,: 'Oh, July's the month they dump us in / The good old Square and Compass Inn, / Where Mrs Newman knows our needs / And gives us really monstrous feeds, / That by the time we're leaving Worth / We have increased so much in girth / That all the friends who know us cry, / We will come with you next July./ To that most heavenly spot on earth / The Square and Compass Inn at Worth.' They look like art students, each carrying a flat bag suitable for a drawing pad, one with an easel.

That cartoon holds history, too. Florence, at the door in a long apron, holding up a steaming tray piled high, is labelled 'Mrs Newman and food'. Charlie stands beside a black and white dog, Benny. The single-storey stable block, separate in a 1916 drawing, is fused to the main building. Perhaps Strong & Co made alterations after buying the plots in front of, and behind, the pub. A horse, 'Ethel', looks out of the stable door. The pub sign bears the words 'The Square and Compass', undecorated by any logo or picture.

Beck's cartoon of 1927

The book records one last famous figure, the pianist Harriet Cohen, for whom Arnold Bax, her lover, wrote most of his piano music. She left a suitable entry: 'Charlie Newman's Cider is never… ' and added the musical symbol for 'flat'. Did she ever come at Christmas? Then, there would be performances of the Worth Carols, written by John and George Corben, who quarried at Gallows Gore and who played them on their fiddles. Each year they were sung, in parts for tenor and bass, in The Square, but I never recall hearing them. Luckily, Sybil Sheppard of Langton transcribed them in the 1950s and they were performed in Swanage at Christmas 2006.

The visitors' book fades out early in the 1930s, but it remains a fascinating glimpse into an era. Sadly, it was not followed by another.

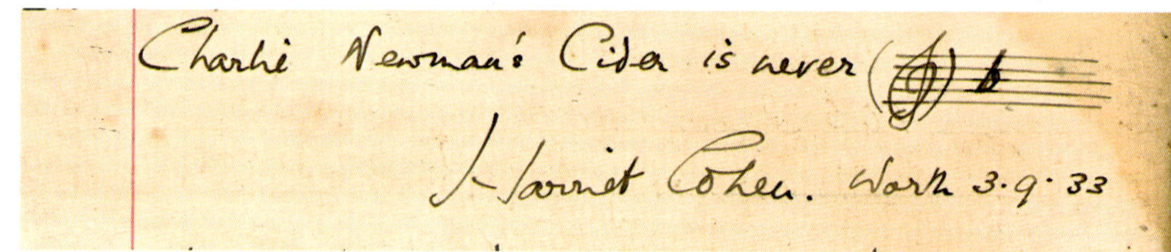

Harriet Cohen's guestbook entry

The lead-up to another war – Old Charlie & the 1930s

During the winter and weekdays, the pub flourished on reliable local stalwarts – Bowers, Buglers, Landers, Millers. Some had their own pewter tankards, others used the then-standard fluted glass ones. They came to wet their thirst after work, to play shove ha'penny on the long board which was Charlie's pride, came, also, for such events as Coastguard meetings. It was because Charlie was the doyen of the Worth Coastguards that the first telephone in the village was set up in the pub. When Colin James' brother and his mate went to The Square of an evening, they would leave a pint down by the wall so that the Worth policeman, William Welsh (a Londoner who lived in London Row), could take a sly on-duty sip.

Hypocrisy was deeply engrained. How many young married couples who stayed at The Square were actually married, how many featured under their real names? Anyone versed in French literature would feel a trifle doubtful about M Charles Swann and Mmlle Odette de Crecy of Meseglise, France, Proust characters, who stayed in May 1932 and wrote 'Jouissance ajoute au desire de la force.'

Shove ha'penny, perhaps with Ambrose Bower and village bobby Bill Welsh

LEFT TO RIGHT
Not named, Freddie Adams, Not named, Harry Samways, Den Bower(?), Sam Bower, Jack Corben, Charlie Newman, Not named, Frank 'Micky' Bower and Billy Winspit

CLOCKWISE FROM TOP LEFT

Ambrose Bower; setting off from the village pond, for a day out in the Daimler bus; Worth posse, from left to right: Burt Grant, Harry Gale, Freddie Adams, not named, Den Bower(?), Frank 'Mickey' Bower; Charlie James with cat and dogs

OPPOSITE FROM TOP

1935 drawing by F. Paterson (also oddly dated 1919?); Charlie Newman in one of many postcards from the 1930s and '40s; John Crabb's father, Reg Crabb, who flew in one of Cobham's planes from Verney Field

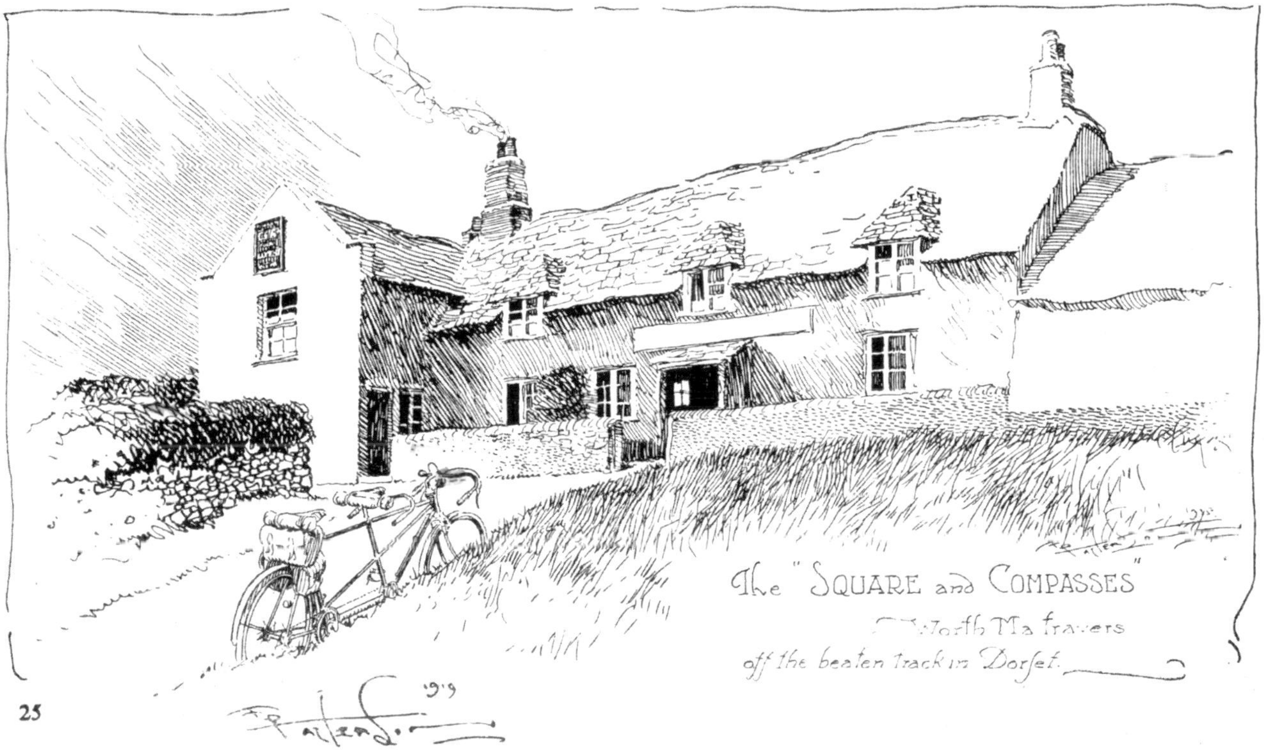

The "SQUARE and COMPASSES"
Worth Matravers
off the beaten track in Dorset.

25

WORTH FARM
DAIRY
LJ 9985

SQUARE AND COMPASS, WORTH MATRAVERS.
R.A.P. Co Ltd
London E.C.4

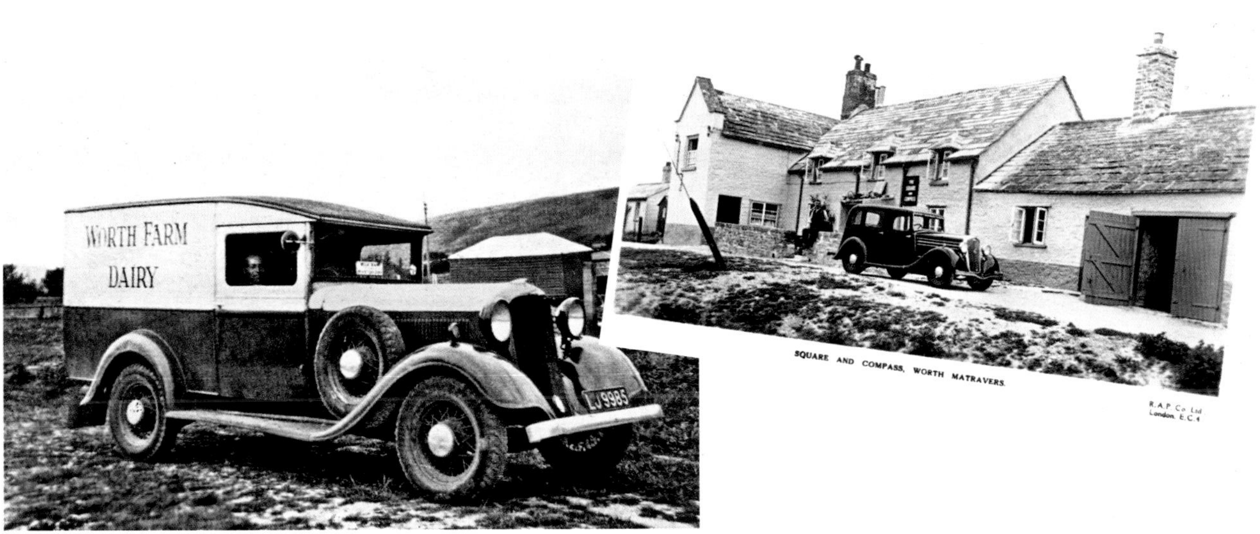

Only one voice documents the scene from the villagers' side. Brian Bugler lent me his grandfather's novel, 'Bachelor's Knap'. Eric Benfield uncomfortably crossed the Great Divide between the Worth folk who worked the stone or farmed the land and the outsiders, for most of whom they featured merely as part of an attractive rustic scene. Would he have published anything but for the contacts The Square and Compass gave him? Two of his books, 'Purbeck Shop' (which Brian republished in 1990) and 'Southern English' became regional classics. Benfield, a quarryman, was born in 1900 and worked in an underground mine at Townsend, Swanage before moving to Worth. Married with three children (the eldest, Hazel, being Brian's mother), he lived in a cottage, now gone, beside the road from Abbascombe to the pub, which he frequented. There he collided with the artists and urban intellectuals who vacationed in Worth. There, also, he met Kathleen Wade, another writer, who carried him off to Basingstoke, where he spent the rest of his life, teaching stone carving at a mental institution and writing his books. He also made an Anti Air-War monument in Wood Green.

Published in 1935, 'Bachelor's Knap' is a thinly-veiled satire on Worth (Here called 'Buttery Corner'). His Worth '...tolerated strangers, but except for the few that had direct interest in them there was no friendliness. The soul of the village was in the fields and hills around. It was not on view to every man and woman that could arrive by car and flash evidence of a box of wealth.'

Told from the viewpoint of Walter Udy, a London artist in search of rural subjects, who arrives on the advice of fellow painters, it relates the mystic conflict between two centres of power. A white-witch figure, Jessie Frome, (is she Wade?) living in the only thatched cottage in the village, is a figure of unrepressed goodness. The force of evil is Tom Player, landlord of The Figurehead, a public house overlooking the village. Tom Player is so transparently a parody on Old Charlie that Benfield is obliged to describe some very un-Charlie features, to distance him from his creation. Tom, unlike Charlie, is large, bald and bloated.

The strongest account of Old Charlie is that given by the articulate tourists. An amusing man, an entertainer, a good conversationalist. It was his character, they say, as much as the attractions of Worth that drew urban pilgrims to his door. But Benfield doesn't like Tom Player at all. He is the outsider from Sturminster Newton, belonging to neither camp but keeping on good terms with, and fleecing, both. 'There was nothing Tom Player liked better than to orate about a guest in his house.' Of Walter Udy, Tom says that he is '…an artist who is going to paint our village in spring. Many do in summer. He'll show the birth of everything.' In fact, 'Tom Player was sure all artists were mad, and if his house had been full he was content to let them be mad together… they spent a lot of the evening talking about things he never wanted to hear…' He was interested when he '…overheard a group talking openly about sex… that's the sort of thing I'd like to talk about…' but '…when he carried in another lot of drinks, he had cleared his throat to tell them a story, and found they were not as free as he thought. They hadn't wanted to hear his stories….'

There is the sinister side of Player. He '…felt he had strings that reached out from him and over each roof. It was like a monstrous spider's web that he could run out upon to gather any prey that was caught.' He weaves his web in opposition to Jessie's powers. The evil at his heart seems to be money, greed, meanness but, as Brian said, Benfield probably owed a lot at the pub. Charlie's grandson, Raymond said of him: "He was very, very strict and wouldn't even trust Father to draw beer in the tap-room. He really trusted very few people. He was very careful with money and successful with it." Player would produce an enormous ledger "There's names there that haven't been off my books ever since I've held this licence, and some that will never be off because they're dead." Older folk, never volunteering the information, when asked, said that Charlie was meticulous over money, almost a miser.

Benfield's descriptions owe little to imagination. His 'Brewer's Day', the first Thursday of the month when the brewer came to take the month's orders and collect his cash, describes a custom of the time. The brewer arrived in an old pony trap, latterly giving way to a car. Quarrymen, seeing him approach, would make their way towards the pub, since he gave a free pint to all present on the day. Then, a pint cost 7d, the same as an hour's pay. The beer was delivered in a horse-drawn dray; Ian Ching's grandmother told him that, as a girl, she sometimes rode up Kingston Hill, beneath the trees, on that dray.

The novel ends with Revolution. A communist intellectual comes down from London and gives a rousing speech on the wall beside the pond. He aims his venom at Tom Player, who exploits working men with his beer, running them into debt. The quarrymen, in search of a free pint rather than a socialist paradise, storm the pub and, throwing Player aside, drink it dry.

Eric Benfield's grandson, Brian Bugler and an illustration by Denys Watkins-Pitchford

Disabled by a stroke, Benfield shot himself in 1955. His most famous book, 'Southern English' (1942), whilst talking of Billy Winspit and Buff Bower, utterly ignores The Square, but it adds another artist to those who visited it. Denys Watkins-Pitchford (1905–90), writing as 'BB' (a grade of shot used in wildfowling), did the book's illustrations, one depicting the Tap Room around 1940. BB also wrote and illustrated my favourite boyhood book, 'Brendon Chase', which told of three brothers running off to the forest to escape school. At its climax, one boy climbs a great tree to take a rare Honey Buzzard's egg. That tale would have resonated with Raymond Newman.

Jessie Frome's 'Thatched Cottage' actually exists. Stone-roofed now, it was one of a group of three beside the church that the actor, Leslie Banks, rented, then bought in the late 1920s. He planned to buy just two but, its thatch in a terrible state, Thatched Cottage stood condemned. Fearing what might replace it, he bought and re-roofed it.

Bank's daughter, Evangeline Evans, has clear memories of village life in the thirties. Her father first visited Worth and The Square during the First War, when stationed at Bovington. The youngest of three daughters, she said that, when supper was nearly ready, her mother would send the eldest girl to The Square to fetch Leslie. He always said 'Have a ginger beer. I'll just finish my pint.' So the first kid sat down happily. Before long, the penny dropped and the second girl was sent up. She joined

her sister with a ginger beer. Evangeline, the last resort, was then dispatched; by now it was serious and he prepared to leave – after, for fairness sake, she, too, had finished her ginger beer.

Banks features in several photographs in Charlie's album, quite apart from the picture on the wall of the Big Room. There is even a well-thumbed cutting entitled 'Fancy Meeting You!' from the Daily Mirror Sept 1st 1932: 'Leslie Banks and Gwen Ffrancon-Davies… both independently discovered the same rural retreat in Dorset, and were extremely surprised one day when they met in the village street… The local innkeeper, an old coastguardsman of much repute, takes a great interest in both the distinguished visitors, and he is coming (to the West End) to see them act on Tuesday.'

Amongst the most prominent British actors of their time, they encouraged Charlie to be naughty. During her early trips to Purbeck, Gwen Ffrancon-Davies coupled visits to The Square with occasional outings to Max Gate, Thomas Hardy's house at Dorchester. There, in his last years (he died in 1928), she sometimes performed for the aged writer. Famous for Shakespearean roles, she died not long ago, having hit her century.

Fancy Meeting You!

Leslie Banks and Gwen Ffrangcon-Davies, who will play the leading parts in "The Way to the Stars," at Wyndham's, on Tuesday, both independently discovered the same rural retreat in Dorset, and were extremely surprised one day when they met in the village street. They had been going backwards and forwards to the place at odd times for nearly [illegible] years before this happened.

Banks has now bought three cottages dating back to the thirteenth century. One of them is known as Lobster House, recalling the old days when lobster selling was a thriving business. The local innkeeper, an old coastguardsman of much repute, takes a great interest in both the distinguished visitors, and he is coming up to see them act on Tuesday.

Mr. Leslie Banks.

To Charlie

Banks, *Daily Mirror*, 1932

'Thatched Cottage' by the Church gate

Un-named woman, Charlie Newman, mystery swimmer and Young Charlie James

Mrs Stewart enjoying Winspit

Charlie had a thing about the bullion on the steamship, 'Egypt', which sank in the Bay of Biscay in 1923. His albums contain photos and newspaper cuttings of its raising, ten years later, the latest showing bullion unloaded at Plymouth. Some must have been sold off, since he acquired that salvaged gold sovereign which, until it disappeared in Eileen's day, was kept in a table drawer in the Big Room.

There are many 1930s pictures in those albums, photographs of anonymous, long-dead patrons. They are often posed beside Charlie on the sitting wall, the sign bearing the pub's name carefully set in the background. Most are couples or young women, although one shows Charlie next to a well-built man clad only in swimming trunks. Some are named – 'Mrs Stewart' on a lilo at Winspit, 'Mrs Walker' and her husband, perhaps, seated amongst the trees at Knoll House, Fridel Meyer in a canoe on a beach. Meyer had a tale to tell: she was a nineteen-year-old German canoeist who, in 1934, set off with her pet Chow to circumnavigate Great Britain. Perhaps the photograph was taken in Swanage. Did she reach The Square? A 1935 cutting from 'The People' shows Bournemouth's beauty queen, Miss Bebe Docksey. His pictures usually have an attractive woman perched somewhere. Charlie had a weakness for women. A toucher and bottom-pincher, most women gave him a wide berth, but tolerated his weakness. Florence didn't. Benfield's Tom Player had slept alone for years and Florence, in her last year, confirmed that Charlie was banned from the bridal bed.

JUNE 16, 1935

THE PEOPLE, 3

BOURNEMOUTH'S BEAUTY QUEEN

Miss Bebe Docksey, Bournemouth's Beauty Queen, who is to compete for the title of Miss Britain.

Miss Bebe Docksey

Gordon Lander, Charlie James and Raymond Charles Newman

German canoeist Fridel Meyer

Their son, Charlie, was quieter than his father, 'more of a dreamer'. He was exceptionally good with his hands, able to create things, turn unexpected objects to use, a repairer of failed machinery. He had an obsession for snakes, too, had a 'pit full of adders' and was accused of putting a sign 'Beware of Adders' on the Winspit Road to discourage trippers. He married the diminutive Frances Burt. They settled in 'Braemar', in front of the church, but now demolished, which his father built for him. Appropriately, his single child, Raymond, was born in The Square, in the room above the Tap Room.

Not wanting to put himself in the shadow of his extrovert father, Charlie started work at Swanworth Quarry, but his asthma was exacerbated by the mixture of damp and stone dust. It was a tradition amongst some quarrymen to work stone through bad weather, dig it in the Spring, then fish through the gentle summer months. Charlie took up fishing and must be the James Newman (he was Charles James) who, in 1929, paid the Encombe Estate a shilling rent for a boat haul at Chapmans Pool.

The village's principal farmer was Colonel Ronald Strange, who bought a large tract of Worth land at Captain Marston's sale after WW1. His brother, Louis, the only pilot to fly bombing raids in both wars, was addicted to the thrill of flying. His rank was confusing: in WWI he rose to Lieutenant Colonel but once in the Royal Flying Corps, became Wing Commander. He was forty when WW II started, but smuggled

Braemar

himself in as a more-junior Pilot Officer, retiring with a DSO, MC and DFC with bar. His legendary exploits included a near fall from his WW I aircraft whilst changing the machine gun's magazine. He kept a plane in a field beside the Langton road, still known as Aerodrome, and enjoyed an occasional beer at the pub. It was probably through him that the famous long-distance flier, Amy Johnson joined Charlie's roll of fame. She was drawn to Purbeck by Alan Cobham's Flying Circus, which performed annually near Verney.

The Coastguard on parade and exercise

In many of Old Charlie's cuttings and photographs, local men pose as auxiliary coastguards, with Charlie as head of the team. The Western Gazette of 14th June 1933

describes a Worth coastguard exercise. "...a good long shot was made by the No 1 of the crew, Charlie Newman, the line falling on the spot allotted with a very tough wind blowing off the Channel." I remember the shock of later Worth Coastguard exercises when living in a caravan in St Aldhelm's Quarry, silent of a calm night. Suddenly, utterly unexpected, a rocket would hiss over the van, aimed towards a pole they'd set up just outside the fence. It took a minute to recover.

The coastguard cottages at St Aldhelm's Head were sometimes let out when Jo Lawrence first visited Worth in 1933. Her father, a naval officer, rented one for six months so Jo, then twenty, soon got to know The Square. For her, the Tap Room was also called The Kitchen. She responded well to Charlie as an entertainer and showman since, by the end of the thirties, she was principal dancer at The Windmill. Later, she taught dance in the Corfe studio which had served Francis Newbery and Frances Hodgkins. Dancers were welcome at The Square. Charlie would come outside and perform a clog dance to entertain everyone, which explains the inscription on a late 1930s photograph in his collection. A run-of-the-mill star's portrait, it shows a dark, very camp-looking young man who signs as 'Paul Anton 26/5/38', inscribing it 'To Charles. You're a better dancer than I am.' But there is more of the spirit of the times. The print names a studio, Willinger, in Vienna, so he was probably a refugee dancer. But, when scanning the picture, Jack noticed JEW indented heavily, viciously across the photograph, written in ballpoint, the ink failing to run.

Jo Lawrence remembers Charlie in front of the pub, always a 'presence', raggedly dressed but radiating charisma. Florence held him on a tight rein, when so inclined. If she thought he'd been away from the bar too long, she came out and called him in. He was scared of her. She rarely appeared, but stayed in the residential section, now the museum, at the end of the corridor.

Later, Jo married John Lawrence. His parents, A.J. & Kate Lawrence, bought Happy Cottage in the 1923 sale, expanding it from the little 18th century alehouse, The Rose. A regular visitor was A.J.'s sister, Edith, a good painter and on the fringe of the Bloomsbury set. She settled at Donhead St Andrew with Claude Flight, another painter, and experimented with the styles that punctuated the developing 20th century. They also pioneered lino-cut printing. Their London studio, with most of their work, was destroyed by war-time bombing.

WORTH MATRAVERS

DRILL AT THE COASTGUARD STATION.—Rocket apparatus and life-saving exercise drill was held at St. Alban's coastguard station on Saturday, under the direction of Captain Buckle, R.N. District Officer, Swanage, and Chief Officer St. Alban's Head. The volunteer crew was promptly on time, and the carts were soon on the spot and every man at his job and post. The rocket machine was quickly got in readiness and a good long shot was made by No. 1 of the crew, C. Newman, the line falling on the spot allotted with a very rough wind blowing off the Channel. After the exercises the heaving cane was won by R. Cobb and G. Millier. It was a lovely afternoon and many visitors witnessed the drill.

Western Gazette, 14th June 1935

Dancer Jo Lawrence

Dancer? Paul Anton

LEFT TO RIGHT

Charles Bugler, Nelson Burt?, not named, George Miller, Eric King?, not named

CLOCKWISE FROM BELOW

Colonel Strange's bi-plane; Charlie and guests; Charlie with Pat Brown; with Durnford headmaster Chris Lee Elliott, on the far right; and finally with a fond friend

CLOCKWISE FROM LEFT

Actress Margaret Rawlings, Charlie and friend; sketch by Elliott Seabrooke, painter and actor, work held by the Tate and Imperial War Museum; Bloomsbury?; and F. Copeland's postcard of The Square and Compass

After a summer day at Winspit, the younger Lawrences and their friends gathered outside The Square at 6pm. Naomi Brooke (then Mills) remembers the mornings. On fine days, they walked to Winspit for a swim before breakfast, the pub's bathing facilities being primitive. Lit by a glass-chimneyed oil lamp, each room was provided with a washstand, a bowl set in a tripod metal frame. Eileen brought a jug of hot water for washing, but it was a poor apology for a proper bath. The ladies' lavatory, reached through the kitchen and out into the courtyard, was shared by all the guests. A pot under each bed served for emergencies. I bet Eileen emptied that.

Eileen was the mainstay of the business, working hard and long for the guests. She cooked and served their large breakfasts, observing a strict gender division for eggs: men had two, women, one. Chickens, wandering through the stone-flagged corridors, were a feature of the pub and probably had been since the 18th century. They appear in some of the early sketches and photographs and merit mention in personal accounts. John Hall, whose mother bought The Haven from Old Charlie in 1936, describes them with conviction as Rhode island Reds, providing fine brown eggs. In summer, they couldn't satisfy demand and, every Sunday, Billy Winspit appeared with his 'nitch of eggs' to supplement them.

Much like breakfast, dinner and tea in the Big Room perhaps?

Gordon Sutcliffe sketch showing chickens in the foreground

Shove ha'penny

Old Charlie and Bryan Brooke – note the U-Boat warning poster

Naomi camped at Hill Bottom in 1935, with friends, including her future husband, Bryan Brooke. They ended each day at the pub, where that photograph of her and her sister clinches the date when the Big Room became big. From then until the outbreak of war, Naomi and Bryan stayed whenever possible at The Square, or at one of the Newman empire's cottages. Her first thought on the declaration of war was that their holidays in Worth were at an end. Gamely, she gave me copies of her 1930s letters to Bryan, saying "You lot thought you'd invented it." It wasn't hard to work out what 'it' was. A problem they had to consider was how to share a bed without anyone guessing. When in adjoining rooms, each had to remember their official room so that, having returned to decent solitude in the early hours, Eileen would bring the right breakfast to the right person. Two eggs to a girl would be a dead giveaway!

In August 1939, planning their holiday, she says 'I will write to Mrs Newman and see what rooms she can provide. I think it is a pity to break our good reputation if it can be avoided. It might mean we can fit in less often and with greater difficulty... I hope she will reply quicker than she usually does.' Did Bryan suggest they share a room instead of flitting from one to the other? A week later, war looming, Mrs

Newman replied. Making her way from Devon to Worth, Naomi writes 'The Fates do seem to be on our side at the moment – we have actually got the Inn to ourselves!' That holiday over, so was peace.

A letter from January 1940 shows that Bryan was playing shove ha'penny with Charlie, accompanied by pinches of snuff. Naomi closes 'With all my love to you, and as much as you can spare to Charlie, bless him.' Next month, she writes. '...I shall have to go (to The Square) for part of the Easter holiday, even if you can't get off. I shall cycle down! The thought of Canon Cove shining in the sunlight, is haunting me… And I want to see Charlie again.' She went down with a girlfriend and sent Bryan a card of Winspit; it is late March and they are just off to 'Canon Cove' for an afternoon siesta.

The Pushman's Post Office

There was rivalry between Charlie and the Pushmans, who held Worth Post Office and also had rooms to let. Most people preferred Charlie's places since the pub was more convenient and more fun. Naomi's last letter was written in March from The Square, although she was staying at Pushman Cottage, 'I have not reminded Mrs P that I've stayed there before and I don't think she's recognised me. I've no doubt she'll remember you, however, but whether she'll also remember that you slept with a woman remains to be seen!' She ends 'Just going in to dinner', so she ate at the pub. Oddly, she remembered no meals, apart from breakfast! When the phoney war became real, their visits stopped. With marriage and babies, one form of romance gave way to another.

The Square's most striking image – Leon Heron's cartoon of Old Charlie in the Tap Room – dates from this period. Labelled 'Got to be Cruel to be Kind', Charlie is shown running from the pub, gripping his crotch and waving a mop. Heron's small caricature of Charlie's son, also Charlie, hangs on the opposite side of the doorway. Leon Maxwell Heron, known as Max, settled at Scoles Gate in the late 1930s with a dark woman, Mimi, but left no trace there, save for many bottles and a grave in the garden. A heavy drinker, always short of money, his paintings were lodged with probable creditors. In lieu of rent, his landlord acquired much of his furniture and some pictures. One sinister image shows a man in a dark back street, another, a Colonel Blimp figure in pink riding a fox.

A Heron cartoon, 'On the Road to Ruin', hangs in The Greyhound in Corfe. It depicts a row of cartoon men (their names on the rear) gazing at the wrecked castle.

A popular image, 'the Heron Girl', failed to keep him solvent. By the time war broke out, he was a shambling eccentric with a large wolfhound, perceived by local kids as the archetypal German Spy. In the garden, lost in undergrowth, is a large grave inscribed 'Wolfie 1933–1950'. His wolfhound? Oddly, dogs caused Heron and Eric Benfield to cross. Hazel Bugler, Benfield's daughter, was out for a walk with her parents and their pet Jack Russell, Tammy, when they met Heron. He offered Benfield, then unemployed, 7/6 (some 40P) for the dog. To her grief, he accepted.

CLOCKWISE FROM TOP LEFT
Leon Heron's work: 'Tally Ho'; Charlie Newman, unknown, Tommy Cooper and Patch-eye Hardy; in the shadows; 'On the Road to Ruin' with Desmond Graham, grocer Tommy Cooper, unknown, butcher Tom Budden, Father Wiseman and Alfie

Heron, at The Square almost every night, had an enormous voice. Jo Lawrence says he fitted into no category, a big man with a round face, happy-go-lucky, full of laughter. He had a funny, old, open, rattling car and would sing 'You are my heart's delight' very loudly as he drove back from The Square down Kingston Hill. 'He and Charlie together were absolutely riotous.' A couple of his funny postcards remain in Charlie's collection, one showing men perched at a bar, the other, a pink elephant looking amiably round the doorway into the Tap Room (unmistakably at The Square), to the astonishment of a seated man, whose pipe leaps from his mouth.

As the thirties advanced, aided by illustrious connections, Charlie Newman hit the media, becoming a pioneer of television on November 3rd 1938 in a programme called 'Picture Page'. Four months later, he was interviewed on the popular radio programme, 'In Town Tonight'. He kept the printed questions he would be asked on television, prompts for his replies and a list of The Square's famous guests, including Gloria Swanson, Amy Johnson and Josie Collins. His pub, he declares, is 14th century! Finally, he gave a song and dance performance. A photograph in the Big Room showing him, smartly suited, at the studio, is signed by Elizabeth Cowell; she was one of two 'hostesses', both from impeccable cut-glass backgrounds, who appeared on prewar television. The system closed down during the war, many of its technical workers being employed on radar work. Perhaps some ended up in The Square.

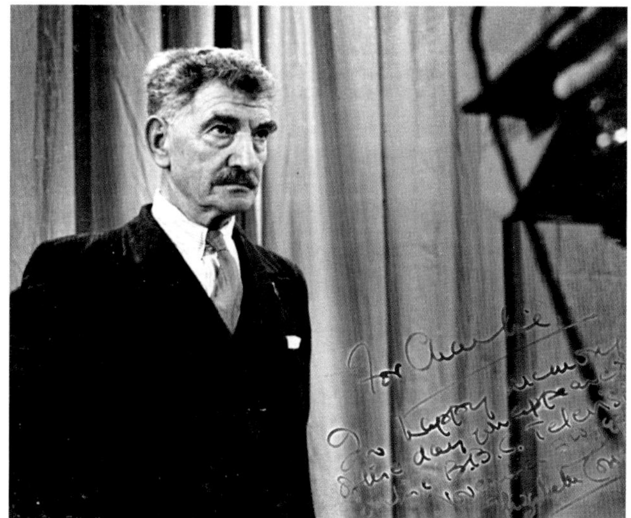

Charlie's BBC televison appearance on November 3rd, 1938, signed by presenter Elizabeth Cowell, far right

Interview with Charlie Newman of Worth Matravers, Dorset.
Picture Page, 3.II.38. 3.30

Q. Well, Charlie, how's Dorset looking ?

A. ...

Q. It's good of you to come up specially. Still beating all comers at shove ha'penny ?

A. ....

Q. You've welcomed quite a lot of famous people down at Worth haven't you ?

A. Yes..including Leslie Banks, Harriet Cohen, Jose Collins, Amy Johnson, Gloria Swanson, Gwen Francon Davies etc.. also artists including Augustus John (pictures)

Q. How old is your inn by the way ?

A. (14th century)

Q. So there should be some good smugglers' tales connected with it ?

A. (story)

Q. Who are your regular customers today ?

A. Farmers, coastguardmen (one myself - long service medal) and quarrymen.
Quarrymen - Purbeck stone - very old quarries
family traditions ~~as quarrying~~ as quarrymen
names of a few
songs composed at their work with the chisel

Q. Are you a singer yourself ?

A. Yes..in choir 25 years..

Q. What about a Dorset song ?

A. (one taught me as small boy...song and dance)

Q. Thank you..... .

Television 1938
London ~~Diamond~~
on the air

Questions for Charlie's television appearance

A large photograph shows The Square crowd at Easter 1939. Some folk can be identified. Bryan Brooke and Naomi Mills are there, as are John and Cecily Walker, and his brother, Harry. So, apparently, are Lord Phillips' parents. Lord Phillips of Worth Matravers is a rarity, having risen to his present eminence as Lord Chief Justice of England and Wales despite remaining a regular visitor to The Square.

That Easter weekend must have oppressed poor Mrs Oliver, at Compass Cottage. In 1939 she wrote to Strong's, making 'various complaints about the noisy behaviour of some of your (Charlie's) customers, especially week-ends in the summer months.' Probably, she was not the first, certainly, not the last to voice such complaints.

Quietly, local folk continued to dominate the place. Billy Winspit walked up from Winspit most evenings, little fazed by the weather. I doubt he ever carried a torch. Other quarrymen and farm-workers came from nearer at hand. The coastguards, stationed at St Aldhelm's Head, had the longest walk.

The Banks family never went to church in London but, when in Worth, each Sunday the girls lined up in pretty frocks and followed their parents into a favourite pew for 11 o'clock Matins. Charlie Newman, who never missed, always arriving at the church gate, smoking. He carefully stubbed out the cigarette and lodged it in a crevice between two stones, ready to light up again when he left. He sang all the hymns very loudly and followed the service with care – until 11.35, when he pushed his way out of his pew and shuffled out. Then, cigarette relit, he hurried back to The Square ready to welcome the Sunday punters. Meanwhile, Eileen taught at Sunday School.

Evangeline Evans, then ten, remembers the outbreak of Hitler's war. She sang in the choir, who wore scarlet cassocks. That day, the vicar's wife crept into the church through the side door behind the choir and handed her a note for the vicar. It said 'We are at War. Pray!' So they did.

A great family man, Leslie Banks was to sail to New York on 4th September to appear on Broadway. He booked Mr Blake of The Castle Inn at Corfe to drive him to Southampton. As the liner pulled away, a fellow passenger told him that was to be the last transatlantic service for the duration of the war. Realising he would miss Christmas with the family, he insisted they get him back on shore. Being a star made it possible. Once on the dock, he rang the only phone in the village – The Square and Compass – to tell his family he was coming home. As he drove back into Worth, he was confronted by a sign across the road reading 'Welcome Home Leslie'. Charlie's work!

OPPOSITE
Crowd in front of the pub, Easter Sunday, 1939, by Murray Hardy. This photo was produced for the advertsing department of Leyland Paint & Varnish Co.

Known present include: John Glover, Bryan Brooke, George Batterbury, Donald Wilson, Naomi Mills, Barry and Vicky Peters, John and Cecily Walker and brother Harry Walker

War again and the end of an era: Old Charlie (1939–53)

And so for the replay. Would The Square fail in Our Finest Hour? Already things were happening nearby. One of George Carter's first jobs, as a teenager in 1938, was to help with digging the trench for the electric cable to Weston and beyond, by-passing the powerless village. A large area south of the road between Weston and Renscombe was surrounded by high barbed-wire fencing; inside men constructed huts and roads to link them. He had no idea what it was for. New technology was in the air and, briefly, Worth was at the forefront.

War brought a major cosmetic change. The pub's walls, long whitewashed, making for a distinctive landmark, were repainted mud-brown. It looks odd in contemporary photographs. From July 1939 until 1970 there was a register of guests, probably fulfilling a legal requirement. It had none of the old book's individuality; just giving the basics: name, address, room number, length of stay. In late September, one of the first guests after the outbreak of war, R. Brutton signed in, never suspecting that, sixty years later, his granddaughters, Juliet and Leckie Haysom, would serve behind the bar.

Even this book isn't untouched by the new war. In 1940 three French soldiers

This Licence expires on the 31st December next.

DOG LICENCE. 7s. 6d. QN 007584
(NOT TRANSFERABLE.)

† FLORENCE NEWMAN
of SQUARE & COMPASS in the
Civil Parish or Township of WORTH MATRAVERS within the
Administrative County* of DORSET
is hereby authorized to keep **ONE DOG** in Great Britain, from the *date hereof* until and including the *31st day of December next following;* the sum of SEVEN SHILLINGS and SIXPENCE having been paid for this Licence.

Granted at Swanage at hours minutes m. o'clock this 28th day of January 1939
by

SWANAGE 20 JA 39 DORSET

NOTICE.—Any permanent change of address should be notified to the County or County Borough Council in whose area this Licence was issued.

Penalty for refusing to show this Licence to any duly authorized Officer, or Police Constable, or for keeping a Dog above 6 months old without Licence £5.

† Insert full Christian Names and Surname IN BLOCK LETTERS.
* If the residence is within a County Borough strike out "Administrative" and insert "Borough" after "County".
P.T.O.

SYMPTOMS OF RABIES IN DOGS.

Change in the manner and habits of the dog, which becomes unusually affectionate at times, but at other times shows a disposition to snap at persons to whom it was formerly attached. Avoiding light by hiding in dark places. Gnawing and eating indigestible substances. Alteration of voice, the ordinary bark being replaced by a peculiar howl. Difficulty of swallowing, but no dread of water. Sometimes ropy saliva will be hanging from the mouth.

In the furious form, these premonitory symptoms are followed by paroxysms of excitement on the part of the dog, with a tendency to attack any animals or persons approaching it. Frequently the dog seeks every opportunity to escape from its home, wanders about snapping at any object which comes directly in the way, continuing its march until it finally drops and dies from exhaustion.

In dumb rabies the lower jaw drops. The dog remains quiet in some dark place, paralysis of the hind limbs soon sets in, followed by death.

Dogs showing any of these symptoms should be at once isolated till a Veterinary Surgeon can be called in.

Any person having or having had in his possession or under his charge any dog affected with or suspected of rabies is liable to a penalty under the Diseases of Animals Acts if he fails to give notice thereof with all practicable speed to a police constable of the district.

The Newman's 1939 dog licence

The pub with full camouflage and overgrown grass

Aunty Eileen with Nanny Jesse Pitts, supporting Raymond's war effort

– fresh from Dunkirk? – stop by, naming their regiments and writing 'Vive le Patron, Charlie Newman. Many thanks to English people.', 'Vive l'Angleterre.' and 'Meilleur souvenir de l'Angleterre.' From the Fall of France until 1945 the register is sparse. Of the few guests during this period some were from the forces, others probably concerned with the experimental work at Renscombe. Fuel was short, the South Coast was restricted and the book was regularly checked and signed by William Welsh, the village policeman.

Until Blue Birds flew once more over the White Cliffs of Dover, Worth Matravers was a sensitive area. Around the coast of Britain CH (Chain Home), a series of primitive radar stations, was set up. At the outbreak of war, this extended westwards along the south coast from Ventnor, Isle of Wight. One new station was near Renscombe Farm and staff from a centre at Dundee and elsewhere moved there in May 1940. Harry Bisby cycled the 85 miles from Bristol to Swanage in a day, then continued up to Worth to take up his post. They were joined by an aircraft equipment team. Amongst the important developments achieved at Worth was the development of a single aerial to transmit and receive. Whilst developing radar technology, their mission was to warn of approaching aircraft. Soon many were approaching.

Suddenly Worth was the centre for a large number of young staff, scientists, RAF and WAAF personnel. The RAF personnel were housed in the camp, but

RAF photos of TRE (Telecommunications Research Establishment)...

...and Worth, with the pub top right

Hooper & Welsh, the village shop

Un-named gunner with Lancaster bomber

Eddy Bowen, Hanbury-Brown and Alan Hodgkin

scientists were scattered around the area. For many, urban men, rural life was quiet. The Square and Compass, referred to by the scientists as The Sine and Cosine, offered light relief. Some lunched there, others took sandwiches out on the cliffs.

On the 7th September 1940 there was a false invasion alarm and the local Home Guard assembled at The Square. It must have presented a formidable sight. Meanwhile, village life continued, overshadowed by the Battle of Britain. Billy Winspit, who boasted he'd never slept anywhere but Winspit cottage, walked up to the pub to face a very different clientele. Charlie welcomed the new arrivals with open arms and those who remember the period always comment on his friendliness.

Examining reconnaissance photographs, the Germans became suspicious of these new encampments. Tall pylons within the perimeter south of the road were constructed of timber. The tallest, rising north of the road above the huts now housing the Adventure Centre, was of steel. They raided the Ventnor station in summer 1940, and Worth suffered hostile action. A fighter strafed the camp and planes returning from raids on Bristol dropped left-over bombs. One hit the RAF cookhouse, killing two cooks. Raymond, then a boy, seeing the planes coming in, jumped into a horse trough beside the Winspit road and from there saw the explosion.

A different clientele of potentially famous men frequented The Square in those summer days of the Battle of Britain. Artists, swept away by war, were replaced by scientists. Bernard Lovell, knighted in 1961, spent the war working for TRE (Telecommunications Research Establishment): "The Dorset Coast in that Spring of 1940 seemed exotic after the snow and ice of South Wales. My pleasure at that move was enhanced by the proximity of The Square and Compass to which we frequently retired during the following months as the German aircraft soon began to harass us… Like all who made the acquaintance with The Square and Compass I have the happiest memories of the reception we were given." Alan Hodgkins, later recipient of a Nobel Prize and a knighthood, was a regular customer, but not all the newcomers patronised The Square. Dr Penley recalls only one visit during his Worth posting.

During the winter, little Raymond Newman came back from Langton school to find his grandfather baking potatoes in the embers of the Tap Room fire, a pail of chicken-feed beside him. When they were ready, he'd share them out carefully 'One for the pail, one for Ray, one for me.' Ray's dietary eccentricities were soon apparent. Hazel Bugler, who ran 'Hooper & Welsh', the shop in Calico Cottage,

remembers him coming from his home across the road, clutching a penny, to ask for, then devour, an Oxo cube. That taste for salt lasted – he loved salt fish and even salted his salted peanuts.

The war affected rural life through alterations in routine: blackout, the rationing of my childhood, with those dull little books of 'points', and restrictions of access. Prior to the fall of France, the holiday atmosphere of Purbeck continued, sailing boats still dotted Swanage Bay and the young scientists swam from the beach. But there were sea defences – barbed wire, mining, concrete hutments and pillboxes, dragons' teeth and gun emplacements. After France fell, private boats were controlled and the piers were cut. The Halls held their cottage until 1942, so John remembers the Observer Corps, who had huts near Seacombe, attending wartime meetings at the pub. A kid of twelve, John found Old Charlie intimidating, a bit gruff.

That summer of 1940 was beautiful, so some scientific staff would go to The Square and sit on the wall, eating their sandwiches with a pint of draught cider. Sometimes the air-raid warden cycled past in his tin hat, blowing a whistle and shouting "Take cover!" No one responded. Rarely, the clear blue sky was cut by arcing vapour trails as distant young men fought for their lives. More rarely still, a plane screamed steeply earthwards, trailing a flag of smoke. John Kendrew, later knighted and joint winner of the Nobel Chemistry prize, talks of an unexpected visit. He was flying over Purbeck when his pilot made a forced landing at Worth, on the field known as Aerodrome where Louis Strange kept his plane. "I remember then having lunch at The Square and Compass with the pilot – cheese and pickled onions and cider, which I hope is still obtainable there."

Martin Ryle, later to become Professor Sir Martin and joint winner of the Nobel Prize for Physics, was more precise about one incident "About mid September 1940 I took my lunch sandwiches to The Square and Compass for some cider and company. On my way back..." a large formation of more than a hundred German aircraft "...flew over – one was hit by Hurricanes and came straight down engines full on, to hit the sea just off the cliff." Another time a Messerschmitt 109 was shot down near Worth and the pilot captured.

Colin James, who farmed at Renscombe, said that the radar folk used to take beer back to the establishment, then dump the crate of empties outside the pub. Charlie gave them credit for the empties but soon discovered he was paying more out on

Original OXO tin

Raymond's first of many bikes...

...and another three-wheeler

John Gilson's photograph of TRE, Worth Matravers from the West Tower

returned empties than he sold bottles. Some local entrepreneur was emptying that crate and returning the bottles one by one to the bar at a neat 2d (those great old pennies) a time.

Meanwhile, primitive tests of crucial new equipment carried out around Renscombe and St Aldhelms Head bore fruit. A crude pulsed system produced echoes from the row of coastguard cottages and Reginald Batt was set to cycle over the rough plateau with a tin sheet reflector attached to the bike, which Bernard Lovell (not then knighted) was able to detect with the new apparatus. Lovell was among The Square clientele, so perhaps it was cause for some hush hush celebration there!

The British/Canadian raid on Dieppe, albeit a disaster, indicated how vulnerable such coastal sites were. German seizure of the developing technology would be catastrophic. This, in part, caused the sudden shift of TRE far inland to Malvern. The Square's place at the forefront of scientific development was brief – a mere two years – but it was crucial.

The end of radar development was not the end of the radar station. The RAF remained in the camp through the fifties before the place was finally abandoned and demolished. At its peak, a large number of RAF & WAAF personnel were stationed there, working in shifts. John Gilson, posted to Renscombe in 1944 and set to man one radar screen, recalled that the transmissions were synchronised with a station on Bulbarrow so that all the pulses were the same. He watched for irregularities in the green traces on a cathode tube, but spent many evenings in The Square, remaining a regular ever since. He also climbed the westernmost timber pylon and took a photograph of the camp with his box Brownie. Far in the

LEFT TO RIGHT
Fan, Francis, his mother Julia and Maud, Billy's sisters

background, The Square is visible. Later, he made a forlorn attempt to persuade Raymond to revamp the place and drag it up-market.

VE Day brought celebrations, but no one remembers much about them. The only trace is the letters 'D Day to VE Day', scratched into one of the tables in the Tap Room. Clear, glaring, when I first drank there, they are so faded now that Young Charlie had to point them out. One of Billy Winspit's sisters lived in Florence where she was married to a painter, famous for an image of the Angel of Mons. They had been out of contact all through the war, so she went up to the first British soldier she saw and handed him a letter to post to Billy. "That's funny" he said "We've just been posted there!" He must have been in the huts at Seacombe. Another snippet: A regular post-war customer from the village, Leslie Turner had a pet nanny-goat, which followed him everywhere. She would even sit with him in the Tap Room, but only once, at Christmas, did she join him in a pint.

We explored the RAF camp in 1960, just after it was abandoned, when demolition was about to begin. The empty huts smelt of damp and decay, but some had paintings of local scenery on their walls. The great wooden pylons were felled, the timber reused in local buildings, but the tallest, steel one stood until 1976. Trev and I climbed it shortly before it was felled, inspired by Raymond's ascent with Mary, then thirteen. The view was amazing. A few days later, as I approached the top with my camera, Pete Cuff, the dairyman, yelled ferociously at me to get down. Foolishly, I obeyed.

John Gilson learned a new craft in front of the pub. He was a pipe-smoker, as was Old Charlie's son. In a time of post-war shortages, with pipe bowls particularly scarce, he caught the younger Charlie carefully adapting a lobster-claw to serve

← CUT OFF CLAW
PIPE STEM CEMENTED INTO END OF CLAW.

Pipes were scarce during the war and Charlie James made them with hollowed out lobster-claws and a box of loose pipe stems. John Gilson (whose drawing is seen above) used to sit with him in the lounge while he made them

the purpose, working it to fit neatly on the stem, then gluing it in place. Gus Smith, Raymond's best friend, remembers going out fishing with Raymond and his father. They left at 5am and he was seasick immediately. It was a hard school and he had to suffer till they went back three hours later.

The younger Charlie, a beachcomber, once found two 50 gallon casks of claret. The customs seized one, but he angered his father by giving sanctuary to the other. One cruel blot stains his character; several people comment on the tricks he used to play on his sister, Eileen, whose life was tough enough in any case. As a conductor on Southern National buses, she always worked with one driver, Fred Burridge, as they drove to and fro between Swanage and Wareham. She often had to cycle to Swanage early to report at the depot. She also had a motorcycle, a BSA Bantam. Sometimes, he let down her tyres, sometimes hid her bike.

Eileen's BSA?

Raymond went to Langton School until he was fourteen. Known as Titch, he was a good footballer but did his best to steer clear of lessons. He and Gus would persuade Mr Peart, the headmaster, to let them do 'coal duty', which, working slowly, meant a day out of classes. There was competition for the job,

Raymond with Sally and right, Eileen Newman surrounded by Swanage bus group in Joan Muspratt's photograph

but they made persuasion a fine art, Gus cycling down to Mr Peart's house to volunteer for the work. It was wartime, and the older kids each had an allotment near Gypshayes. Every year, Raymond, who loved gardening, won the competition for the best patch.

In Spring, after school, Raymond and Gus went through the undergrowth along Drove, in Langton, bird-nesting, a legal pursuit until 1954. As he grew up, Raymond's father encouraged his interest in egg-collecting. When the boys were about thirteen, the three of them would go 'up cliff' after Guillemot, Razorbill and Puffin eggs. There was rarer prey, too. Passing Winspit Cottage, Billy, who kept a sharp eye on the cliffs whilst out fishing in his boat, would shout out where the peregrine and raven were nesting. Once they reached a site, Charlie would fasten a rope around his son's waist, then send him over. 'Get down, then, and don't be long!' Ray always wore a black beret; with the eggs in the side of it, he would put it on his head and climb back up the cliff. He was not supposed to climb without his father.

Later, they went egg-collecting with another man who had a small motorcycle with a characteristic pop-pop-pop motor: they called it 'Mousepower'. That, then

Peregrine by Mary Dwen

Winspit Cottage and Raymond out egg collecting

The Dutch Girls, here with a younger Raymond and Old Charlie

The Parliament meets: Amos Bower, Fred Ingram and Fred Cobb

a car, opened up the surrounding country as far as the New Forest. Ray also had a Douglas motorcycle, which they enjoyed taking apart. And there were other distractions: they both noticed the two Dutch sisters, Groenwald and Eden Rie, who stayed at The Square from time to time in the late 1940s.

After the war, Nina Warner Hooke and her husband leased the little shack on the corner, neighbouring the younger Charlie's bungalow, Braemar. She wrote of November 1st 1948 in her book 'Seal Summer'. Charlie had put down a new net, borrowed from Percy Wallace, in Chapmans Pool. The wind got up as the day advanced, so Charlie returned to the slipway, hoping to save the net from the rising sea. Another fisherman, Maurice Lane, offered to help him.

The net was not far from the shore. They reached the first float and Maurice steered the boat whilst Charlie pulled it in. Everything happens so fast in an accident; it is hard to recreate reality. Some say the net caught on the bow of the boat so that, when the next swell hit, it was pulled under and turned over. Others talk of a massive freak wave rising from below, throwing the boat in the air and hurling the two men into the sea. Both men, good swimmers, set out for the shore, but Charlie suddenly gave up. Perhaps he had an asthma attack. Lane got hold of him and swam in, a difficult feat in a calm sea, much worse when it is rough. He made it to the rocky western shore and was helped out by Sid Lander and Charlie Hooper. They sent young Alan Lander for the doctor and tried artificial respiration for an hour. It was already dark when the Hookes drove down with Frances, his wife, but there was no hope.

Charlie was dead, aged 42. Frances, a shy person, stayed clear of the pub, taking work at two of Langton's prep schools. Charlie's death came as a terrible blow to his elderly father. It was worse for Raymond, then seventeen: part of him died with his father. For eight weeks, he kept to his house.

When Leslie Banks died in London, in 1952, they brought his ashes down to be buried in Worth churchyard. His daughter, Evangeline, was amongst the mourners. When he saw where the ashes were to be buried, Old Charlie turned to her and said "Well, he's beside young Charlie. He'll be fine there."

'The Bystander' from 1935

Charlie visiting 'The Fox' in Corfe, perhaps Shrove Tuesday

"Beer Is Best"

And this is Leslie Banks, less murderously inclined than he appears to be every evening in "The Two Mrs Carrolls"; he's drinking a toast with Charlie Newman, host of the "Square and Compass" at Worth Matravers. —

And Mr L. Jellineck preserves a judicial attitude behind. —

Happy memories of 1935 and a close friend

Alvar Liddell, the broadcaster, visits Billy Winspit and Rhoda Bower

Business flourished, boosted, no doubt, by the post-war prosperity of Swanworth Quarry and the re-opening of Winspit Quarry by Bob Harris, who set up new machinery there. All the production, coming up the track by lorry, passed The Square. Old Charlie's popularity continued, too. Among Worth's visitors was Alvar Lidell, the famous wartime radio broadcaster, who also used to do voice overs for training films for the radar research team. The Lidell family would take a cottage and from there visited the pub and Billy Winspit's cottage.

Bob Harris' lorry was used to ferry Worth LSA 'Life Saving Apparatus', then Sam James' tractor took over. Charlie and, later, Raymond were both auxiliary coastguards and both were awarded for completing 35 years of service. In 1949, (one of Charlie's pencil notes on a flyleaf commemorates the event) the coastguards moved into fresh quarters at Weston. Four years later, on a foggy February night, a new Chief Officer, Ernest Pye, came to Worth from Lancashire. His son, Doug, then ten, remembers their arrival by bus in Worth. Were they with Eileen? As it was late at night, they put up in the pub rather than trying to settle into a cold cottage and he had to share a bed with his father. Ernest Pye slipped easily into Worth life, becoming a regular at The Square and one of the men who sang.

Charlie kept pigs, but slowed down as he grew older. His last beast, an elderly sow, died in 1949 while on her way to Wareham Market in a Morris van. He recorded her passing in another pencil note. He kept busy till the end. Ken Miller, along with his father and friends, had his first drink in the Tap Room in 1951. Someone bought a round at the hatch but when Ken stood to get another, his father pulled him down and tapped the table sharply, whereupon Charlie came in with the second round. He would still do a little tap dance there on occasion. Some say the table tapping explained the name Tap Room, although it is a common name for a room where beer is served from the cask. Certainly, there was lot of tapping around.

Charlie died on Sunday November 15th 1953 in Swanage Hospital, aged 82, and was buried at Worth. After long service as an auxiliary, he was borne to his grave by fellow coastguardsmen. All of Worth was there, including Stella Smith, destined to marry Raymond. There were representatives of Lloyds Bank (which had done well out of him), Swanworth Quarries, the RAF station, Southern National Bus Company and the Purbeck Lodge of Oddfellows. The vicar, Revd Payne, quoted Charlie: "If I could live my life over again, I'd follow my own footsteps." That makes a good epitaph. The Swanage Times mentions his prowess at shove-ha'penny; he won his last local tournament in 1947.

The brewery, Strong and Co of Romsey, left his widow, Florence, in place. She held the license but her daughter, Eileen, did most of the work.

Some of Old Charlie's earlier pigs

Eileen on horseback – the Newmans have always kept animals

Women's work – Eileen in control (1953–1973)

Another Humane Society bronze medal holder is District Officer George Pawson. His district—Swanage.

Daily Graphic article, 11th October, 1949

Hero of many rescues and Royal Humane Society bronze medallist — Coastguard Percy Wallace.

Percy Wallace, self-appointed Mayor of Worth Matravers

Initially, Eileen was more familiar in her role as a bus conductor than as a publican; there were few women conductors in the 1950s. But she had grown up in the pub. As a child, she sometimes woke in the night and crept down to peep through the little spyhole on the stairs to see drunken men lying on the floor and against the tables, fast asleep. She wasn't alone. Decades later, during holidays in the 1950s, two sisters, Toni Bernardy and Sue Hampton (nee Prior) used to watch shove ha'penny from the same vantage point when they were supposed to be in bed.

Eileen was a plain, quiet woman who often wore her hair in 'headphones' over her ears. According to pre-war guests at The Square, she did the lion's share of the work and got little credit for it. Her father overshadowed her and she was treated badly by her brother. There was a romance, so they say, when she was on the buses, but that ended unhappily. The job gave her some independence from the pub, but her mother became ill, developing terribly ulcerated legs, one of which had to be amputated. To make life harder, Florence went blind and was confined to her rooms, now housing the museum, before dying in August 1961. She had one treat: Esme Prior, working at the Dorothy Bakery in Swanage (and particularly generous with penny bags of 'stales' for us schoolboys), brought her a dough cake every evening.

Always an unselfish support to her parents and their business, Eileen had to give up the buses to become a full-time publican. Raymond helped out, but he had his own work. Asthma saved him from National Service, so he took a job at 'Burt's Nurseries' in Swanage, which supplied the greengrocer, 'Erica', with vegetables and flowers. Then he started landscape gardening with Dick Burgess before working for a time with Gus Smith. Part of their work was grave-digging (Gus dug his first grave when he was thirteen), which is how Raymond dug a grave next to that of Lawrence of Arabia at Moreton. They also built Worth's bus shelter.

Eileen's reign was crucial. During her time many hitherto-traditional pubs succumbed to a make-over, remodelling their interiors to create a 'modern' environment. The Purbeck, one of the busiest in Swanage during the 1960s, and The Scott Arms in Kingston were prominent victims. Their little, ill-lit rooms were united into large spaces laced with pseudo-rustic decoration. Eileen, despite suggestions, refused to alter The Square. Had she succumbed, it might have attracted

more custom during the lean sixties, but what of the long-term charm of the place? The only major change was the removal of a brick fireplace in the Tap Room; in the mid fifties Leslie Linnington replaced it with an ugly stone one.

The atmosphere changed with Eileen at the helm. Unlike her father, she was not a personality to dominate the evening, but she had been an active presence since the thirties. The locals and the holidaymakers were familiar with her as a generous, sympathetic landlady. The coastguards still met there and all their formal group photographs were taken in the Big Room. One, from around 1954, shows them after receiving a trophy for the quality of their drill. Many of the faces are familiar from my early drinking days.

The coastguard in the Big Room, in rough order from back row: Ted Bartlett, Charlie Hatchard, Bob Bugler, Arthur Prior, Edwin Bray, Paddy Gillespie – next row: Nelson Burt, C. Mead , Roy Cobb, Ted Miller, Tommy Bartlett, Ray Newman– front row: Charlie Hooper, Reg 'Joby' Cobb, Earnest Pye, 'Taffy' Davis and Harry Samways

Amongst the regulars, Pat Brown used to walk up from Acton with his little terrier. After he died, I squatted in his cottage, which had neither electricity nor running water (well, there was a tap in the garden). His wartime ration books were still there and a calendar for 1938, overlooking me as I write, shows the coronation of George VI emerging in a 'thought-bubble' from an ancient wireless. Pat drank Guinness. Eileen would get a dozen-bottle crate for him, which he often finished in an evening. Several of the quarrymen drank heavily. Fred Bower could put down sixteen pints then walk home.

Billy continued to walk up from Winspit. There were rowdy singsongs in the evening, with Paddy Gillespie, a bus driver, playing his accordion. Billy's speciality was the fiddle, which he played left-handed. Later, on television, Rolf Harris plugged a new instrument, a Stylaphone. Ron Bower bought one, and Paddy accompanied it on the piano. Trev Haysom recalls Geoff Hooper, late quarryman and poet, coming to work at St Aldhelm's Quarry with tales of such sessions. Much of the repertoire was drawn from the music-hall and, apparently, 'Flinger' Bower was fond of singing a ditty with words like "Flip-flap up the Channel with a whitewash brush." Some of the singers, including Ken Riman, only opened up at Christmas. Perhaps that was due to the 'Royal', a special strong beer, which Eileen ordered in for Christmas.

Billy Winspit

Pat Brown and Percy Brown with the Dutch Girls

Kevin Keates, who owns a quarry at Worth Gate, came regularly in the late fifties. He was 8 or 9 at the time. When his father had changed and eaten after a day at the quarry, the family often went to The Square. Kevin was left outside on the bench by the door with a soft drink. He didn't mind it in the summer, when there were holidaymakers' children to play with. Out of season, it was deadly boring. He could hear Paddy singing to his accordion inside but was supposed to stay out. He was not altogether abandoned. Georgie Bugler ('a lovely man') used to stand in the entrance of the porch smoking his pipe – he favoured Erinmore tobacco – and chat with him.

George Bugler

Often, the folk inside sent out glasses of something less innocuous for Kevin. On a good evening he might get a couple of bottles of Guinness to drink surreptitiously. Georgie might treat him to bitter lemon – he used to order a 'Bitter 'n' Lemon'. Georgie lived alone in a spotless wooden place at the end of London Row and he wanted a budgerigar. Kevin, who kept budgies, gave him one. It became the most spoiled bird ever, with a choice of all manner of seed to eat and its cage filled with every type of avian convenience. Anne Gainher gave Georgie a tankard to join the others behind the bar, which Eileen returned to her after he died. She has it still.

His great nephew, Brian Bugler, reckoned there was method to Georgie's favouring the doorway of the pub: he would greet holidaymakers very affably, offering them a drink in such a way as they felt obliged to offer him one. A neat diplomat! According to Billy Norman, he always said "I'll have a small Special with you." By the end of a busy evening he was often unsteady, so Billy would give him an arm homewards. Later, both Brian & Charlie took on the task.

One Christmas – 1957 or '58 – all the regulars put money into a kitty and bought a bottle of everything to pour into a bucket, creating a formidable punch. By the time they went home, all were in a terrible state. Kevin remembers having to help carry his brother-in-law. One of the quarrymen stayed behind, draining the last dregs of the bucket and, so the rumour went, actually drank himself sober.

Eventually, Eileen stopped taking guests. There are no entries in the register after 1970. Before that, several names appear regularly throughout the year, people who became familiar with the locals, some settling in the village.

From June 1946, Commander Chris Schofield signed the book every few months. (The Woolley family appeared about the same time.) Usually alone, he developed a fixed pattern, always staying for a fortnight in November and another after

Gwen Woolley, Alison Viney and friends

Christmas, when the place would be at its quietest. His breed was exterminated by the obsession with stranger-danger. He was fond of boys but, as one of the boys who gained from him, neither I nor any of my friends ever complained of any untoward advances. A botanist, he was an expert and his speciality was fungi. When I was about ten, he took me on the heath at Arne and pointed out unusual plants, including Whorled Carraway. Recently, I looked it up and was reassured to find that it exists.

Schofield settled in Worth, living up the road from the pub, surrounded by books and clocks; his ambition was to get all the clocks to chime together. Seeing Kevin Keates looking bored, he took him home, showed him his butterfly collection. Later, he gave him a copy of the Collins Guide to 'Birds of Britain and Europe', one of many excellent wildlife books that came out in the 1950s. Kevin also had a fact to remember: when he bought a pair of binoculars the diameter of the object lens must be three times the magnification.

Schofield socialised more with summer visitors than with locals. He was a depressive, quiet man, perhaps intimidated by us folk; he never gave any indication that he knew the boys he'd befriended when they became adult. He was obsessed with time: 'You could set your watch to him.' He came when the pub was emptiest – midday and early evening – sometimes disappearing behind the bar when people came in, rather than face them. Otherwise, he sat silent in a corner of the Tap Room, with his own half-pint tankard, a silver christening mug. So quiet was he that my diary one day records his 'Thank You' when I held the door for him.

He was tight. When he told him to keep the penny change, Raymond Newman nailed it beside the bar as a rare souvenir. It remains there. He ate half a packet of nuts with his drink, then left the rest behind the bar for next day. Ray had another cause for bitterness: after Schofield moved to a nursing home, he measured the contents of his mug and discovered it held more than a half-pint. Over the years, Schofield had profited by gallons of beer.

In the late fifties and early sixties, Anne Gainher (now Powys-Lybbe) stayed regularly, along with her son, Jeremy Hogarth. She came to Worth in the mid '30s with her father, a surgeon in Weymouth, then signed in as Col & Mrs James Gainher in 1954. An attractive woman, she favoured dark clothes, whilst Jeremy liked army surplus gear. In the summer, they emerged early, she with a cigarette, and headed

Anne Gainher with son Jeremy Hogarth and dog…

…and good friend Eileen

for Winspit. She became very fond of Eileen, helping her behind the bar or washing up when things got busy; she continued to visit until Eileen died.

Anne mentioned Harry Samways, who worked on the farm for the Stranges and lived in a little cottage, now much transformed, at Weston. He was often at The Square, where he used to play the piano and sing. It was said that, over several weeks in The Square, a London couple befriended him as part of their summer holiday, inviting him to the big city. When his vacation came, he responded by walking to London and turning up on their door-step. The welcome he received was unmistakable, so he walked sadly home and spoke to no one for some weeks afterwards.

Harry was averse to water and rarely changed his clothes. It was a great charity when we offered him a lift whilst driving back from the quarry. He lost the key to his cottage and for several weeks had to climb in and out of the window. Finally, he had to go to hospital and came to Eileen beforehand, very worried in case they gave him a bath. Eileen was sympathetic, but thought they probably would. It was good that they did, since they found the key undisturbed in one of his boots. He had a poetic line to him, comparing rooks on the telegraph wires with the crotchets of music. Sometimes, on sunny days, he fell asleep on the roadside bank, half across the road. The road to Renscombe turns sharply across the front of his cottage. Heather Strange (now Elgood), given it when she married, christened it after him Old Harry.

Billy Winspit had his own corner of the Tap Room and he had a crate of beer under his seat. An intelligent, sensitive man, he passed all his life at Winspit.

Billy Winspit sculpting…

…and outside his workshop

His three sisters all moved away, two abroad. Anne spoke of him taking off his boots to reveal a beautiful pair of white feet, faintly blue-veined. How incongruous that is with my image of Billy! He philosophised, too, saying of the Cold War "Them Russkies will scratch the stars from the skies". Several people tell the Christmas tale of Billy turning up at the pub and producing from a sack two cats he had carved. He handed them to Eileen, wishing her a Happy Christmas. She smiled and thanked him, whereupon he clarified the matter "That'll cost you £5".

Sometimes Anne's visits overlapped with those of George Willing, a games' master at a school near Shaftesbury, who drove down on his motor scooter. In the Special Operations Executive during WW II, working behind the lines in France, he spent most of his holidays at The Square. When I asked Anne if she was also in the SOE, she replied "George Willing and I did strange things during the war – we agreed never to talk about it, even to ourselves."

At The Square, Willing spent much of his time clad in tracksuit and gym shoes, helping Eileen out with odd jobs. Sometimes, he and Anne biked down to Swanage for Eileen's shopping, "no dreadful hats in those days." He stayed in "a small house, near the geese" and some say he worked for his keep. More probably, that was just

George Willing and Anne Gainher

George and pail

the way he liked passing time. Signing the register in a tiny, clear remarkably-undeveloped hand, his name leaps out from the page. In March 1962, he was killed when the scooter skidded near The World's End, Almer on his way home from The Square. He drank little but, according to a newspaper report: "He enjoyed being with the locals' said Mrs (sic) Newman.' Perhaps, if he'd worn one of 'those dreadful hats'…

Jim Chambers and Tony Buffery, both long-haired before the fashion had really taken hold, were geologists connected with the Natural History Museum. Initially, as students in 1961, they camped out in Purbeck. Later, nearer to solvency, they put up at the pub. In search of ancient evidences, they would turn up at St Aldhelm's Quarry; once even left a sign on its gate claiming, inspired perhaps by a Square breakfast, that it was infested by 'giant green frogs'. Cdr Schofield, they felt, saw them as part of the National Decay. To enhance that suspicion, they once paraded past him with a Union Jack flying upside down.

Later, Jim came down with his American future wife, Sharon, who found restrained English breakfast conversations at The Square quite irresistible. A phrase lifted from a neighbouring table, 'Wheels within wheels, so to speak',

Jim Chambers and Tony Buffery

Sammy the Seal

its context long forgotten, became a potent addition the family's vocabulary. Tony was responsible for a major technological introduction into Purbeck. He affected beagles and one of the beasts wandered at the end of the first extendable lead ever seen here! He also pointed out, no doubt correctly, that crescents of rocks appearing at low tide at Chapmans Pool, Egmont and Punfield Cove were caused by the weight of slipped land pushing up an arc of sea-floor.

Within a year, two individuals emerged mysteriously from the sea. In 1961 Sammy, an Atlantic Grey Seal, settled happily at Chapmans Pool. He was extraordinarily tame, sitting out on the slipway ready to swim across and flop up the beach to greet any newcomer, seizing their hand gently in his mouth. Sammy became famous and brought trade to The Square. As for Frank Honour, you can choose your version of the great wreck of March 1962. Joan Begbie, ever charitable, described the 'Sand Dart' as victim of a terrible storm, a miracle anyone survived. Joan should have known; she appears in several c1960 photographs of the pub façade, though I wouldn't have thought her a drinker. As I recall it, the miracle was that the night was calm, if foggy, but the ship tried to cut across St Aldhelm's Head, rather than take the conventional route round.

The 500 ton 'Sand Dart' wrecked on St Aldhelm's Head

Whatever the truth, the 500 ton dredger travelling up the Channel lodged firmly on the rocks just west of the tip of the Head. Perhaps it was high spring tide. There she stayed, rusting and beaten by the weather, until the high tides of autumn allowed her to be dragged off. I cycled out there on my birthday, 10th March, a couple of days after the wreck, the first of a number of visits. Nobody bothered to salvage much of the goods on board. I had the exercise book that served as her log (Young Charlie has it now) and we removed the distress flares, which formed the highlight of a party later that year. As for the crew, they dispersed homewards: all save one.

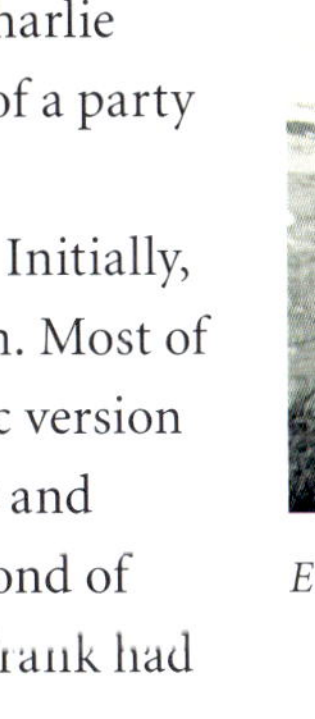

Eileen and "that dam cat!" (Si)

Truth to tell, Frank Honour probably went home, too – but he returned. Initially, he was supposed to keep an eye on the ship, so he rented a room from Eileen. Most of the rest of his life was spent around The Square and Compass. The romantic version of the story is that he and Eileen fell into each others arms in a mist of roses and violins. No one who knew them well felt that was the situation. They were fond of each other, perhaps it was love on Eileen's side, but they were never lovers. Frank had a romance soon after he was cast ashore, but it was not with Eileen.

Frank was the ship's engineer, apprenticed at Rolls Royce and useful with his hands. After settling at The Square, he gave Raymond the keys to the ship's store,

Eileen and Frank

Cockeye and Sherry

Frank Honour

which was full of red and green paints. From then onwards, every job Ray took on involved persuading the customer of the glories of green (or red) paintwork. He settled in a shed near White Lodge and did odd metalwork jobs. Rumour claimed that he made the wrought-iron gates to Arundel Castle.

He drank deeply into the pub's profits, but Eileen appeared not to care. Sometimes, he overdid it. Basil Stumpe found Eileen weeping over the assets of the Thrift Club, which had disappeared just as they were due to be paid out. Basil lent her the money in return for credit. Since he drank heavily, the debt was soon cleared.

Frank was large and florid, with small, insecure eyes. Some men found him threatening; more liked him. One man said of him "A bloody rascal, but then I like rascals." His side-kick was a Dobermann, Hans, while Eileen had a couple of collies, Cockeye and Sherry, and a beloved Siamese cat. At first, Raymond accepted Frank as a fact of life and the three of them sometimes went out along the cliffs together. Frank developed his fondness for drink, finishing the evening with what he called a 'heart-stopper', created from a mixture of different spirits, lightly laced with fruit juice. Gradually, Raymond, who often worked with Eileen, began to begrudge the depredations on the pub's assets. He blamed Frank, grew increasingly hostile to him and, in October 1968, moved away, taking the license of The King's Arms in Langton.

In the sixties, the regular summer visitors frequenting the pub included the Brookes, who bought the row of cottages at Weston in 1949. There were three daughters, Marion, Nicola and Penny, who attracted other folk to frequent the pub, including Doug Pye, son of the coastguards' Chief Officer, and my brother, Anthony, who married Gail, Marion's best friend. The Phillips came often, as did the Woolleys. Victoria Cross (nee Woolley) saw Eileen's rule through a child's eyes. She and other children were confined to the Children's Room, in the projecting museum wing, which had sparse furniture and a little black and white television. Eileen was, for her, 'a very austere spinster who hated children' and the kids were 'scared stiff of her'. When Ray moved to The King's Arms, the Woolleys shifted their loyalties there.

Shandy I

The locals often played darts, the board then set up left of the Big Room's fireplace. I don't remember playing myself – I was never any good – but my diary shows that I did. Notable amongst the regular players was Pete Cuff, the dairyman. He was remarkable not merely for his ability but for a special ritual, recalled by

Basil Stumpe, Jo Lawrence, Stella and Ray Newman at The King's Arms

Winter 1963

everyone from that era. Staring hard at the board, he held the dart at belt-level, rotating it several times before actually throwing it. Whatever the magic, it worked.

The first months of 1963 were memorable. A blizzard was followed by a long drop in temperature. Even in Purbeck, with heavy frosts deep snow lay for weeks. John Burt, the postman for Worth, had to walk from Acton Gate every day, with snow banked high either side of the road. He remembers Eileen as 'wonderful', giving him breakfast every morning. There was a limit to the houses he could reach. By the time he was ready to return, other folk had gathered at the pub, waiting for a lift out of the village on the milk tractor. Anne Gainher helped Eileen take a sledge-load of supplies down to Winspit Cottage. Trev and I waded out to the quarry a couple of days after the snow. Did we stop at The Square? I forget.

The doyen of local customers, Billy Winspit died in 1966, to be commemorated by his carved, oft-chipped cliff-stone cats in the Big Room and the portrait in the Tap Room. When first put up, not long after his death, that painting caused consternation. Bright and gaudy, it contrasted cruelly with the rest of the décor. Time and nicotine have mellowed it to old masterdom. A good likeness; one of Stumpe's best. There are more of his paintings in the Big Room, including portraits of Eileen, and Raymond in a mysterious miasma of cobwebs. But there was method to Basil's art – his brother, Brian, took many excellent portrait photographs from which Basil copied, even, at times, traced.

Billy Winspit, Rhoda and Pippin

Basil Stumpe portrait of Ray Newman

When Worth was sold, Billy Winspit refused to buy his pair of cottages: 'We built them. Why should we buy them?' but he persuaded the Lawrences at Happy Cottage to buy them and paid rent. When he died, Jo Lawrence, who had inherited the place, went to ask his widow, Rhoda, her intentions. She had no wish to stay on alone. To her surprise, Jo found that Basil Stumpe was renting the smaller cottage. One thing led to another, and they married and settled at Winspit. Basil was very regular – too regular – at The Square, he and Frank becoming close drinking partners. He painted no pictures there, merely got drunk then came home to paint against a background of loud music. Jo grew to hate the pub, once a pleasant part of her life. When they moved away from Worth, in 1971, it was mainly to get Basil away from its malign influence.

The Square always drew underage drinkers. Bill Norman used to go in at sixteen, in the late 1940s, and, given a half pint by Old Charlie, was told to sit quietly. Then, most of the other men were from the quarries. Eileen found it hard to place youths she didn't know age-wise, so a lot of underage drinking went on. My brother, Charlie, used to go up by motorbike with his mates, including Peter Chambers and Bruce Bamber. They would get tanked up on scrumpy (10d-4P – a pint in my early days) then drive back erratically through a helmet-less world. Now an Australian lawyer, he asks whether the term 'thinking outside the square' actually refers to The Square. Who knows?

Wetting the baby's head

Diddy Thomas, from Corfe, was into the same game – in fact, it transformed him. He started drinking in The Square in 1964, aged 16, arriving on his trail bike. He would sit yarning with Billy Winspit, who always sat by the fire, and remembers the other old timers in their flat caps. One evening he was up there with some Corfe mates, well lubricated with scrumpy, which they chased down with Lamb's Navy Red Rum (a detail he always recalls).

As they headed home, he was delayed when his L-plate flapped up in front of the headlight. He caught up with the group on the nasty corner ('Cow Shit Corner', some call it) before Kingston, but failed to take it and went straight into a telegraph pole. Phil Lovell, who appeared soon afterwards, covered his face, but his mates protested that he was still breathing. He was, and is, but spent a couple of years off work as they tried to put his leg back together with metal pins. So that is how Diddy got his limp. He sees that accident as a positive event in his life, allowing him to look again at the life he was living and choose another tack entirely. Life is short and he has always interlaced work with travel. The police rebuked Frank Honour for serving him, but it went no further.

Another of the underage gang was Tim Wiggins. Big for his age, at 15 he was able to pass Eileen's easy scrutiny. When hay-making at Renscombe farm with Dicky Bartlett, Ken Miller and Ray Aplin, they would round off the day with two or three pints of green scrumpy – "and it was green!" – before going home. In the sixties, The Square was seen as "a boring pub" but Tim preferred it partly because it was an eccentric, old-fashioned place. He used to go up there with Wendy Hale, his future wife, meeting other couples who frequented the place, including Reg and Esme Prior and Ray and Barbara Bray. The Priors were there most nights.

His parents sometimes brought Brian Bugler when he was a kid; Eileen plied him with ginger wine, which he didn‘t like but couldn‘t say! At least he had a logic for his crimes, reckoning, at sixteen, that if he was old enough to work and pay tax, he was old enough to drink. Logic has little to do with Law. He has Frank tales. Frank was armed, since he mixed with the hunting and shooting fraternity. When a group of Hell's Angels turned up and started trouble, Frank shooed them away, threatening them with his shotgun. After they'd gone, someone asked "Is that thing loaded, Frank?" to which he replied "That's for me to know and you to find out!" A typical Honour aside.

Then there was the shove-ha'penny board. It was sacred. Small holes remain in the Tap Room paving where the legs of the table were set in to keep it firm in Old Charlie's time. The surface was crucial, well-polished. On foggy nights – there are many in Worth – a shout of "Close the door!" rose in unison when anyone entered. The condensation slowed the board! If a ha'penny fell on the floor there was a penalty: was it drinks all round?

There were quiet evenings, that very personal sort when only a few friends were present. Anne Gainher remembered music, Frank and Eileen: "He did give her some happiness, watching them dancing together in the Tap Room, Eileen looked beautiful, she glowed with happiness, and she loved him to the end in spite of everything. She loved him better than her precious cat, and that is love."

I passed the winter of 1971-72 in Worth, spending many quiet evenings in the pub, rarely chatting with Frank. I felt uneasy with him. One evening Eileen commented "Someone‘s burning sea coal". I confessed. A lot of folk must have used it when she was a girl, so she knew the distinctive smell. No one does now.

The age of the Famous didn't end: they merely crept in and out more quietly. In an age before terrorism, the labour Foreign Secretary, Michael Stewart, and his wife came. They ran the gauntlet of the rural Tories, who lined the corridor and made *sotto voce* remarks as they passed. They stayed at the Grosvenor Hotel in Swanage, where I was a sometime waiter, and a helicopter gave us a thrill in 1968 when it fetched him for discussions on the Soviet invasion of Czechoslovakia.

Raymond & Stella move back, then Raymond alone (1973–93)

In December 1956 Raymond married Stella Smith, a distant cousin of Edward Smith, who held The Two Hammers in Worth through the mid 18th century! My first memory of Stella was of a pretty teenager, with her long, fair hair done up in plaits around her head. She worked in the grocer's, Montagu Purchase, and there was an accident. A small boy, I pulled out the bottom tin of a display pyramid of tins to see what would happen. The result was shocking, but she took it all in good part. I never forgot. Both children were born in Worth before the family took over The King's Arms in Langton, Mary in 1960 and Young Charlie in 1966.

In 1973 Eileen, plagued, like her mother, with incurable leg ulcers, decided to retire, moving across the road to White Lodge with her beloved Siamese cat. Raymond and Stella, along with Mary, then twelve and Charlie, only seven, took over The Square & Compass that April. They brought several loyal customers with them, including Roger Brown, who had worked with Ray, and part of the Langton football team. David Sole, a non-drinker who had befriended the family, also became a visitor, encouraging Mary and Charlie to look for fossils.

Stella and Raymond are married, Worth, December, 1956

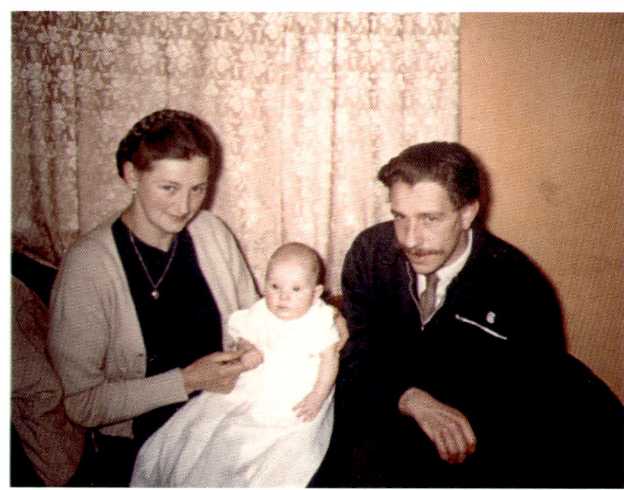

FROM ABOVE
Mary's and, later, Charlie's christening and then together by Channel View

Andrei Daiko, a White Russian from Hongkong and a bright architectural student, who had stayed with the Newmans at The King's Arms, began to patronise The Square. Long haired and with eyes of dazzling innocence, he would persuade Raymond to open the Big Room (that showed charm!), then play Debussy's 'Claire de Lune' on the piano – repeatedly. The only true hippie, untrammelled by reality, his mind wandered happily amongst flowers and songbirds. He lived in a geodesic dome he built beneath Emmett Hill and idolised Keith Critchlow, who had taught him.

Keith and David Critchlow were regular visitors to the village and pub. Keith married Gail, daughter of 'Paul' Crabbe, Britain's first black JP. Paul had discovered Nina Warner Hooke's shed (known locally as Pig'n'Whistle), opposite the church,

and took it on a long lease from Eileen at an exorbitant £26 a year. Coming down from London with her son, she entered The Square only occasionally. David and Muriel's first visit, in 1956, was under her auspices. The Critchlows sometimes borrowed the shed, so their daughters, Emma and Sophie, got to know Mary and Charlie Newman, then living next door at Braemar. Later, Emma often helped behind the bar. Keith and Gail, who spent their honeymoon in the shed in 1957, sometimes rented one of Eileen's two caravans, parked across the road from the pub.

Although already ill with cancer, Stella set about making changes. Muriel Critchlow, suffering the same problem at the same time, gave her some support. Stella involved herself with running the thrift club, planned a second hatch to serve the Big Room and made the first serious attempt to trace the pub's history.

CLOCKWISE FROM LEFT
Paul(ine) Crabbe and son Biff; Nina Warner Hooke's shed – the Pig'n'Whistle and Paul Crabbe and her entourage

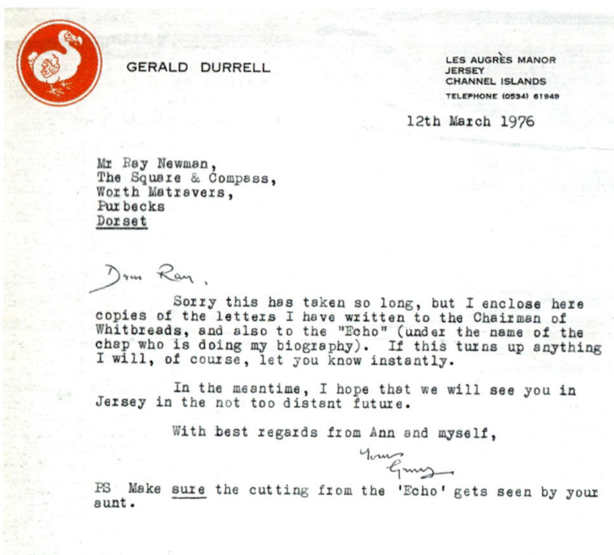

GERALD DURRELL

LES AUGRÈS MANOR
JERSEY
CHANNEL ISLANDS
TELEPHONE (0534) 61949

12th March 1976

Mr Ray Newman,
The Square & Compass,
Worth Matravers,
Purbecks
Dorset

Dear Ray,

Sorry this has taken so long, but I enclose here copies of the letters I have written to the Chairman of Whitbreads, and also to the "Echo" (under the name of the chap who is doing my biography). If this turns up anything I will, of course, let you know instantly.

In the meantime, I hope that we will see you in Jersey in the not too distant future.

With best regards from Ann and myself,

Yours
Gerry

PS Make sure the cutting from the 'Echo' gets seen by your aunt.

Gerald Durrell's letter to Ray

Charlie bottling-up – he recounts stamping on Durrell's sore foot

But she had little time and some of the papers she gathered have disappeared. Luckily, Mary kept many, which proved useful in writing this book. Meanwhile, a letter to the brewers, dated 1976, shows that Ray had already set up his little museum behind the pub. Did a vague letter to Ray from his friend, the naturalist Gerald Durrell, also concern the museum?

About this time, Nick Collis Bird, then Chairman of the Wessex Folk Club, used to bring the club to The Square to play traditional music on the first Friday of the month. In summer, little Charlie would come round, trying to sell them lettuces. Apparently, Stella was indignant about a sign 'No Coaches' at the turning to Worth, saying it was bad for business. Years later, the folk club took a coach down to The Square in her memory.

There were other musicians. Jim Etherington began to perform in The Square in the mid seventies as part of a trio, called 'The Pith and Wind Band', including his brother, Mike, and Jack Rogers (excellent player of bazouki and Irish stuff – a purist). They'd sometimes play in Tap Room, little Charlie collecting glasses. Ray took to their music and often kept things going till 3am.

CLOCKWISE FROM TOP

Stella, Ray's mum, Frances, and Ray; Margaret Kirkwood; Joan Begbie, Ray by Tap Room's stone fireplace

CLOCKWISE FROM RIGHT
Gerald Corbett's stunning image of Ken Riman; and of Ray and Shandy II; Chris Foss's last portrait of Ray

Gwen and George Woolley, Liz Viney, ?, Nick Viney, ?

Tony Buffery and the Woolley's Rolls Royce

Amongst the post-war visitors who always stayed at The Square on holiday were the Woolleys, who came from Leicestershire. George and Gwen had several children. George wore a naval cap, which Billy Winspit described as 'flat as a flounder'. After her husband died, Gwen bought a holiday cottage in 1954 on Winspit Road, first of several, and appeared frequently in the pub. She could not be described as 'low key'. The family manufactured socks, which kept them well-heeled, and Gwen would park her maroon Rolls Royce ostentatiously outside the pub. Once, someone came in to ask for the driver of the Rolls Royce, reciting the registration number, to move. In the late 1970s when a long-distance balloon hit wires near Acton, Charlie was among a mob who crammed into her other car to see it. On the Queen's silver jubilee, she distributed a celebratory consignment of Union Jack socks.

Standing in the corridor, she would hold forth in a raucous voice, which often caused me to divert to The King's Arms. But she had a good heart. Hearing of Stella's illness, she arranged the best treatment available in London, certainly extending her life.

To add to Raymond's problems, simultaneously Mary became ill. Stella died on 13th January 1976. Raymond never recovered. He was brought up as an only child, used to being tended and looked after. He had married for love and, much as he loved Mary and Charlie, he never adapted to his solitary state. Stella was irreplaceable.

★

Throughout his difficulties, Eileen helped Raymond in the pub. Meanwhile, Frank stayed on at the shed, running his metal-work business, firstly from beside The Scott Arms in Kingston, then from a workshop near Prospect Farm. Even when he rented a flat in Swanage, he still wandered in from time to time. When Eileen was running the bar, often he appeared. Estranged from an easy supply of liquor, he was beset by financial troubles. Friends gathered round to bail him out, but drink was hitting his health. Then he developed cancer and Eileen cared for him as he sank towards his end. Eileen died on 8th October 1981, closely following Frank and still speaking fondly of him. She was only 65. Some lives seem unremittingly tough; would she have seen hers that way?

My pre-drinking relations with Raymond were less cordial than with Stella. In the mid fifties, Ray collected birds' eggs, still a common hobby but newly condemned by the 1954 Bird Protection Act. He usually took the whole clutch. Trev Haysom and I, pioneer conservationists, saw him as a threat to vulnerable birds, especially the local peregrine falcons and ravens. While Ray was active, both species usually failed to raise young in Purbeck. He was a remarkable climber, short, wiry and oblivious of fear. We always thought he had a starting pistol to scare sitting birds from the cliff and locate their nests. In fact, he used a little tool he'd fashioned, which discharged blank .22 cartridges. Once, sure that he was carrying a freshly-taken clutch of peregrines' eggs and had to pass that way, we ran to Langton Police Station to get the sympathetic policeman to arrest him. But, Saturday afternoon, he was at a football match. As Raymond and his friends drove past, one wound down the window and said "You boys should be indoors doing you homework." Humiliation!

We kept on visiting the pub after the change of regime, but at first there was an atmosphere. Neither mentioned the egg-collecting issue, but both were conscious of it. Finally, Raymond cleared the air. A diary entry from October 1978, just before I left for 2 ½ years in India: '…got talking to Raymond, who took me behind the bar to see a barn owl he's stuffed full of formaldehyde. He raised the subject of our having always been on the opposite side – he collecting eggs and us trying to stop him.

Ray Newman by Gerald Corbett with Annabel Dean and family friends on bench

THE SQUARE & COMPASS
Worth Matravers

22
THE SQUARE & COMPASS
This famous house stands on high ground in the Purbeck hills, famous for centuries for their marble, and the sign honours the men who cut the marble. The square and compass, still a symbol used by freemasons, are the stone-mason's basic tools. Indeed, until Cromwell destroyed it in 1646, the Ancient Company of Marblers used to meet every Shrove Tuesday in nearby Corfe Castle. Presumably some ale was drunk then too . . .
A series of 25 inn signs. Bournemouth.
WHITBREAD & COMPANY LIMITED
Established 1742.

Whitbread collectable cards

He said that he was now into conservation, too... Then he said "Go up stairs, watch the cat – it's sleeping in the middle of the stairs – and Charlie will show you something." There I found little Charlie in his blue boiler suit and he showed me several drawers of eggs. Raymond came up and started telling me where different eggs came from. Oystercatchers – two clutches he said came from between Freshwater and Kimmeridge – and he told me stories – a trip to Scotland, a mate who broke his back in a fall from a tree, how in the early '60s he'd seen me on the cliff near Winspit, just around the corner from where he, with Frank Honour and Eileen, planned to take some Rock Pipits eggs. He decided "Oh fuck him. I'll risk it" and tied on the rope. He was just about to get over the cliff when Frank tested it – and it parted. It was rotten. So I was nearly in at Raymond's death! I told him of my photograph of him climbing the fir to the sparrowhawks in Little Linnings Wood… Told me about the terrible climb he had to a peregrines near Bat Hd – his worst experience, where he was forced to swing in to the eyrie – found himself dangling and exhausted in mid air. The rope was forty feet too short to reach the shingle and he was too tired to climb up. It took me back to the 'Newman' of the fifties with his beret on his motorbike, black, battered and British…'

For those who only remember Ray as he grew steadily weaker, thinner, it must be hard to visualise him as he was in the fifties. He may have offended us by his egg-collecting, but he was formidable; we admired his guts and ability to climb. For trees, he made himself a pair of climbing irons to attach to his feet, each with a horizontal spike to grip the trunk. He seemed fearless. By the time we called a truce, peregrines had been almost exterminated world-wide, not by egg-collecting but by insecticides like dieldrin. Jed Corbett took several good photographs of Ray with his eggs, one a popular postcard.

The group of local and holidaymaking teenagers of that time included Victoria Woolley. She lists Ross Prior, Jeff Lander, Nobby Norman, Jed Corbett, John Strange and Mary Newman among her local friends, adding holidaying families such as the Critchlows, Brookers, Lloyds and Youngers. The Square was only one of their venues around the village. Later in Raymond's reign, she was fated to meet her future husband in the drinks queue. Victoria describes Raymond as '…a unique character… he always wore the same clothes; a maroon sweatshirt tucked into a grey pair of cords, and suede hushpuppy boots and a copper bangle on his wrist. He had a habit

of smoothing down his hair with both hands and always having a cigar on the go.' She speaks of his knowledge of wildlife and the soft heart that had him knock logs on the hearth before putting them on the fire, to avoid consigning woodlice to the flames; that balanced against his unfurious rages.

Even before his return to Worth, Charlie was up to mischief. Tim Wiggins and Ken Miller, trying to lay a carpet at The King's Arms, were irritated by his running across it, so tied him up in a hessian sack. When they released him, he gave Tim a kick in the shins which still tingles! After the move, Roger Sheppard, sitting outside The Square, looked up to notice little Charlie on the roof ridge. Alarmed, he went in to tell Raymond, whose response was "Silly bugger!" The roof was Charlie's escape route from trouble. Often, when things went wrong, he'd trot off to Reg and Esme's place. Once, Esme entertained him and read him stories, little realising that the whole of Worth was in panic over his disappearance. Another day, he walked into the pub, followed by the first Shandy with a dead chicken in his mouth. Raymond was furious. "I'll teach that dog to kill my chickens" so he tied the dead bird to Shandy's side. Later, she appeared without it. "Have you taken that chicken off, Charlie?" "No. It fell off and she ate it!"

Charlie on the roof

Raymond stopped collecting birds' eggs and concentrated on fossils, laying the foundation to the pub's museum. Many of the saurian bones he collected from the Wealden deposits of Swanage Bay were sufficiently interesting to attract a palaeontologist from the Natural History Museum to catalogue them. David Sole's overriding interest was palaeontology and he spent his spare time collecting fossils then meticulously cleaning them. In the mid 1970s, Charlie tagged along with him, picking up a great deal and turning it to good use. One of those boys who learned more out of school than in it! On rare occasions, David took both kids to Charmouth to search for golden ammonites.

Meanwhile, Raymond tried to balance running the pub, raising the children and following his hobbies. It was not always easy. He liked his drink and would stay up late. The pub hours became very loose; often, I wandered home from The Square well after midnight. Late nights mean late mornings. For 35 years Eva Cobb, living almost next door, gave invaluable support, doing all the housekeeping and, while they were young, getting the kids off to school. Eric and Yvonne Bunny, friends of Raymond's from Southhampton, used to run the pub for a fortnight during their holidays.

Ray with hat acquired from the 'Mayor of Casterbridge'

Mary Newman...

...on the roof

This gave Ray the chance to take Mary and Charlie away. They set off in the car, once only reaching Swanworth before stopping for the night. Ray would call in on the landlords of The Bankes Arms in Corfe, and The Sailor's Return at Chaldon, which delayed a couple more days. Finally, he put his foot down and headed for Cornwall, the true objective.

In the early seventies a new clientele, also destructive to the local cliff birds, began to meet in The Square. Climbing took off as a hobby, and Purbeck drew an increasing number of young men to pioneer its cliff routes. Uncontrolled, they climbed during the breeding season, disturbing cliff-nesting birds. Richard Crewe, their doyen, who wrote a book on Purbeck climbs, often called in with his friends. It was difficult to sustain my hostility to the climbers. Most were pleasant, ready to compromise: a secret weapon was their good parties! Hugh Sandall, who became friendly with some of them, provided the venue for post-Square socialising. Eventually, seasonal 'no-go' areas were agreed. Lucky, since climbers became a fixture; later, some even invaded the area behind the bar. Like Jamie Hannant!

The farm workers and quarrymen customers fell away one by one. Stan Rusbridge, Bill Norman, Ron Bower and Paddy Gillespie still stood in the corridor. Stan and I sometimes talked India, he having served there during the war. He alone smoked Woodbines and when he died Sarah found a stash of them in the tobacco drawer. Pete Cuff was usually there, too, a damp roll-up always hanging from the side of his mouth. There were one or two men in that era who, with or without alcohol, easily turned to violence; one or two who inspired it.

On their father's death, Peter & John Strange divided the farm between them. Their children, David, Heather and Ronnie as well as John and Julia, darkened The Square's door from time to time, some more frequently than others. Then, one after another, they sold up and moved away. Andrew, Patrick and Gerald Corbett, grandsons of the founder of The Old Malthouse, also grew up in Worth and grew into The Square.

Folk musicians turned up occasionally, most frequent being Nikki Hann or Pete Scott, both with guitars, the latter an early boyfriend of Mary's. Sometimes Toby Chadwick played his silver penny whistle, or Pete Jaggard, escaping his role as Punch'n'Judy man, sat down at the piano to give a Schubertian rendering of his Vampire song. Val Quinn would produce his mouth-organ.

Ray was always after dead creatures to submit to the formaldehyde treatment.

As a little girl in the early 1980s, Nico Campbell-Allen came up every day, her mother working in the pub during the holidays. Charlie sometimes took her and Cindy Prior looking for fossils and she was fascinated by the living animals, including Charlie's pet crow, Jim, and a stoat which came after the chicks. Raymond introduced her to dead beasts. He shared his interest in taxidermy with his friend, the naturalist, Gerald Durrell. Ray commissioned Nico to collect any dead birds or mammals for him. To her mother's irritation, these went, well-wrapped, into the freezer, beneath the pasties and pies. In the Tap Room a squirrel and a hedgehog pose immortally in a glass case. One day, just before closing time, Ray came round and, in his customary manner, told the punters to piss off home. When Esme asked why, he said "I want to stuff a hedgehog." Is that the one? A bit drunk and very experimental, he even injected his own thumb with formaldehyde. It turned black and took three months to revive. There were still deep-frozen corpses in the freezer when Raymond died. In the attic, they found a ghastly barn owl, reduced by moths to a quill-covered skeleton.

Both Ross and Cindy Prior worked for Ray when they were quite young. Ross was there, on and off, for ten years. Sometimes he ate with Ray, always coming home to moan about the excessive salt. After closing time, they'd go on outings, looking for bottles, fossils or beachcombing.

Charlie Newman…

It was always difficult to persuade Ray to open the Big Room. The pub had to be packed solid before he succumbed. He just didn't like the idea of all that extra cleaning. He opened it for Coastguard meetings; after all, like his grandfather, he was awarded the medal for 35 years of auxiliary coastguard service. He continued the animal tradition with several cats: Titty Wee and Sooty I. Sooty II outlived Raymond and was, for Sarah, the true pub cat. There was an improbable woodlouse-eating Pekinese, 5 goats, the inevitable geese and chickens. Behind the pub was an aviary, with Zebra Finches and Cockateels. To these Charlie added waifs and strays, those crows, oiled Guillemots and rabbits.

…and 'Jim' Crow

Kim – Clive Kimberly – rolled up from Solihull and, apart from playing shove ha'penny, introduced a metal detector to the scene. Charlie, then twelve, went out with him to search the undercliff at Hounstout; they found a stash of Victorian coins – perhaps from a lost purse. But the great event in Square talk was the Gold Coin, which Kim and Ross Prior found near Chapmans Pool. None of this inspired Charlie to get a metal detector. That came much later.

Emma Critchlow's partner, Jens and Kevin Cross, New Year's Eve

By the early 80s, Jim Etherington and band appeared every other Friday

Quinn – Richard Cranham – began to frequent the pub after fishing at Winspit and Seacombe. He would appear, with or without a girlfriend, and sleep out in some barn or a cliff quarry. He introduced Charlie to a remarkably varied diet, including curries, road kill and bird's eggs. One winter, around the New Year, he turned up with his current girl, and picked up Charlie, then thirteen. They slept out in the army ranges and were due home next morning, but decided to go on to Lulworth. There, the girlfriend got too drunk to drive. When they finally reached Worth, late in the evening, Raymond, frantic with worry, had the police out.

For several years in the 1970s, there was an annual Worth Pram Race to raise funds for Harman's Cross Youth Club – was it on Whit Monday? Revived from an earlier race, it was based on the pub. Reg and Esme Prior always took part, since their son, Ross, was involved with the club. David Sole invariably won.

Another of The Square's annual events, New Year's Eve fancy dress, became a major feature in the calendar. No one is sure quite when it started, but it was well-established by 1990, when I list Val Quinn appearing as a horrid, fat gypsy woman, Diana as Cleopatra, Young Charlie in Rasta gear, Tony Viney as Mr Punch and Jon James and Charlie Lander both in drag. Never into dressing up, I stayed with the mufti crowd. At midnight, the operatic Brian Withers, often a feature in those days, gave us a powerful Olde Lang Syne. Esme Prior claims that the fashion moved from The Square to Swanage. Apparently, Bill Norman's brother came up one New Year's

The Sultan of Worth and heir

Eve and, impressed, went round the Swanage publicans, suggesting they do the same and offer a prize for the best costume. That fancy dress in Swanage became an event of national significance!

Also, briefly, nationally significant, Colin Moinihan, Thatcher's Sport's Minister, would drop in. His visits to the Tap Room once coincided with that of one of the team who made masks for the satirical television programme, 'Spitting Image'. They were duly introduced.

By the early eighties, Jim Etherington was well established and appeared every other Friday at The Square. He was one of few who could persuade Raymond to open the Big Room. The place would be packed, with folk coming from far and wide. Often Brian came with him. Brian, an entymologist, ran a printing business in Wareham. He also sang opera, usually taking the lead for the Durbeville Amateur Operatic Society, based in Wool. The Big Room was often terribly crowded and, if Brian arrived late, he came to the open window. Jim passed the mike out to him and he would open up with popular arias in Italian. Sometimes the crowd had rugby versions, with which they accompanied him.

Often Ray's daughter, Mary, helped behind the bar; she also kept the books. In 1978, she married and moved down to Swanage, but still comes back to the pub each week and always appears, with or without her children, at Square occasions.

Ray on the roof with 'Jim' Crow

Mary, Ray, Ken Woodhouse and Charlie receive another award

Charlie, Ray and Mary

Fred Cobb, Ken Riman, Jack Howell and Ron Bower…

…Len and Doff Mitchell, Ray, Ron Lewis, Eric Bunny, Kevin Andrews…

…and Billy Norman, Christmas, 1978

At some point, Ken Woodhouse stepped in to support Raymond. At least, that was the theory. Neither man wished to take the role of the charming Mine Host. Ray was famous for his unfriendly attitude; largely an act, it became something of an attraction. When people complained of the service, he would direct them to a rival establishment, The Crab Inn at Winspit. When they had walked down the valley to find The Crab Inn was out, they were in no mood to return. Ken lived in Studland and slept little. He arrived at 6 each morning and, after breakfasting on barley wine, cleaned the place up. Then he set about making food, spreading flour liberally around the kitchen. His game pie was very popular, and Sarah still follows his sausage pie recipe. Above all, he was noted for crab sandwiches. Ray rarely got up before eleven, and when he did, they would doze either side of the bar, their conversation limited to "Another whisky?"…"Ummm!"

There was always back-up to clean the pub. Hazel Bugler came in at one time, to find bank notes spread all down the stairs where Raymond had dropped them. (After Raymond died, Charlie found the takings from the previous August at the back of a shelf!) Di Quinn used to tidy up and help behind the bar. Ken even trusted her to make crab sandwiches. They took a morning break at 10. Ken would sniff, "Lovely coffee", then disappear behind the bar to top it up with whisky.

The Quinns moved to Purbeck on Nov 5th 1987 and spent their first evening at The Square. They often needed Hugh Sandall's good nature (and car) to get them

home of an evening. A sculptor, Val was drawn to Purbeck by the stone, met the Bonfields and started work at their quarry. Val liked the atmosphere of the Tap Room, the air of a French café, too small to avoid conversation with strangers. Crowded, too, since the Big Room was always closed. They often arrived with little Tilly, their daughter, who suffered the boredom of our chat before falling asleep on the bench. There were always those who stood in the corridor, whom Steve Coleman, sometime barman, referred to as the 'Outpatients'. They included Heather and Jack Ross, Bill & Marion Norman and Penny Bullock. The Quinns shared a table with Laurie & Dee Baines, Terry and Jean Elson, Pete Jaggard and Wendy Wharam. John Galsworthy, prematurely white-haired and great nephew of the novelist, often joined them. Di painted (and paints), embellishing metal objects with bright floral designs. Raymond commissioned her to decorate an enamel jug, which held eleven pints of cider: the Quinns' favoured cider. She was commissioned to inscribe it 'Muddy boots is better than no bloody boots' and, amongst the flowers, portray the pub. The Handys settled in the village and, later, both their children served behind the bar. Debbie told Raymond that she played the accordion and was touched when he let her play Stella's instrument.

Debbie Handy played Stella's accordion. Also, Charlie's first attempt at a cider press

From time to time the pub hosts wedding receptions. In 1988 Jack Daniels chose the Big Room for the reception for his first marriage. To lubricate the day, Ken mixed up some punch, which must have been fierce. It was one of many marriage celebrations. Raymond and Stella held their reception there, as did, many years later, Dave and Brenda Harris. Around 2000, Steve Warbeck, a composer, had his reception and a pig roast at The Square, the climax of a musical procession up Priests Way from Swanage.

One of Raymond's entertainments was horse racing. On Saturday afternoons – or any other time when the beasts were running – he squatted, or leaned on one elbow, watching a little television set behind the bar. If he was in the way of everyone trying to serve, they could like it or lump it. As his hair and whiskers grew longer, his face faded amongst them. He had his own style at closing time, coming in on the late gang in the Tap Room with "Haven't you buggers got homes to go to?" That was on the mild days, when he was not particularly worried whether they moved or not. At other times, he sent Cindy in to spray the tables with furniture polish. That usually worked but, if no one reacted, another favourite trick was to throw a metal tray down on the floor. That brought an immediate response. Shandy II backed him up with her howling.

'Howling' Shandy II

In early 1989 Sarah Loudoun and Charlie became an Item. Those were Charlie's beret days. At first, they shared the work. Ray and Ken managed the lunches whilst

Dave Harris at the helm

The Tap Room tables with a touch of polish

Ray...

...Charlie, Shandy II, Sarah and Ben

Charlie and Sarah served in the evenings and weekends. Often Ken dozed on a tall stool by the bar, sometimes outside in the sun, where Charlie once placed a dead adder on his sleeping chest. On another occasion, he fell asleep whilst a mass of sausages were under the grill. Unlike Alfred, their incineration did not lead Ken towards kingship. After he retired, Janet made pasties, then food was bought in until Sarah resumed home cooking. Raymond was sick, no longer bothering to look after himself, so she and Charlie increasingly took over running the pub and Tereska began to serve behind the bar.

Charlie's adder on a dozing Ken

For a couple of years after Ken retired, Geoff & Tracey Norwood came to help out. Taking advantage of the newly-liberalised licensing laws, Geoff started opening for the whole day on Saturdays. Normal now, then it seemed revolutionary. Tracey took over the cleaning. When they finished, Charlie's cousin, Dave Harris, stepped in, running the pub when necessary, giving Charlie and Sarah the opportunity to escape the routine. For several summers, Dave Eyles, sometimes helped by Melanie, filled in when there was a shortage of bar staff.

In autumn 1989, a gale blew down the pub sign. Since it was out of season, there was a long delay in replacing it. Meanwhile, Sarah had a bright idea and Diana Quinn got to work to implement it. On April 1st 1990, a bright new sign swung in the breeze. Inscribed 'The Jolly Landlord and The Mad Dog', it bore a portrait of Raymond with Shandy II. Ray examined it satirically, almost grinned, and left it

Di Quinn's sign, April 1st, 1990

The south-facing side

there. It remained in place for some weeks, disconcerting visitors, who searched gamely for The Square and Compass in other parts of the village. Eventually, it was consigned to the Big Room, to be replaced by a sign painted by Donna Glave, depicting the stylised Square & Compass logo that also featured on the pub's matchbox.

The stone fireplace in the Tap Room, which Raymond never liked, finally met its doom. Late one drunken evening in April 1990, Charlie and Ian Ching attacked the stonework. Mike and Simeon Bizley completed the job, opening up the old hearth. In the rubble they found two coins, a shoe and, as Val Quinn recalls, a brick stamped C.N. 1943. A shoe in a fireplace is an old token of good luck. Charlie commissioned Richard Simpson to create the present furnace to replace the old hearth. It certainly works! Meanwhile, Ian set about repainting the interior, using a yellow not quite to Raymond's taste: he wanted nicotine.

Shandy II ruled over the last decade of Raymond's life, barking and howling when he rang the bell for closing time. Her relationship with me became a joke. It started abruptly in the autumn of 1981. After an evening working at the quarry, I sat quietly in the Big Room, which was deserted but for a family party in one corner. Shandy walked in, took one look at me and started barking. That became the pattern: she'd follow me affectionately, then bark continuously. Raymond even gave me chocolate to bribe her affection: she never succumbed. One evening I was smoking in the Tap Room when two keep-fit women came in, talking to each other of jogging and the dangers of Lurking Men. Shandy sidled up, looked at me and growled; one of them looked up and said "Ah! You don't like to see your master smoking, do you?" I held my peace. The barking ended with Shandy's death in May 1992, by which time she was virtually voiceless. An epitaph from my diary: '… she gave me an air of importance… since I could neither enter nor leave without a fanfare…' She was replaced by a similar Shandy III.

In August 1992, Charlie and Sarah put on the first Square Fair, partly a response to the demise of Worth's Fete. Ian Ching produced good posters for those first fairs, most of which hang on the wall of the Big Room, and Oni Wyatt recorded the day in a series of watercolour sketches, one of which graces the Tap Room wall. A tradition of fireworks at the end of the fair continued for some years, but The Square's animals (a powerful vote bank) strongly opposed it. On such busy days and nights, Paul Loudoun

Charlie's freehouse above

CLOCKWISE FROM RIGHT
Eddie Shutler selling scrumpy; Charlie chiming last orders from the roof; Mike Bizley constructs his Square monument supported by Alan Davis

served his locally-reared lamb, pork and venison. Charlie brought in more good music, more often. In fine weather, the music moved outside, but complaints of noise drove it back in.

That summer, the sculptor Mike Bizley produced a massive Square and Compass, fashioned from railway sleepers, which Roy Ford and Alan Davis helped to erect. It remains in place. Mike's son, Simeon, after an excessive evening on a lean pocket, paid Raymond a cheque for a million pounds. It bounced. Mike was one of a small group who arrived under their own steam. He (from Spyway Barn) and Bill Langtry (from Herston) walked along Priest's Way. Charlie Burt made his way from Lower Lynch; Ian Ching and his neighbours came from Quarr; Diane Dumashie cycled in and I walked or cycled from Dunshay. We all had stories. One night, taking the short cut across fields to Gallows Gore, I woke with my back against a taut fence, the bicycle beside me. Miscalculating the position of that fence, both had leaped it!

As his health deteriorated, Ray began to worry about the pub and Charlie's future. The Monopolies Commission decreed that the top six brewers held too many outlets. Whitbread, with 6000, was encouraged to reduce its holding to 2000. It sold off some and let others out on long leases. Ray was offered a 20 year lease, but both he and Charlie decided to hold out for a better deal. After Raymond died, Whitbread suggested that Greenalls take over that block of pubs. They sent a representative to examine The Square. Charlie discouraged him, painting a grim picture of the situation. When Greenalls refused it, Whitbread offered Charlie the freehold. He had six weeks to raise the capital.

In his last days, living on a diet of whisky, occasionally diluted with Complan, Ray became very thin. Finally, hospitalised for something quite different, he caught pneumonia and had no resistance to it. He refused to lie in bed, sitting up in a chair. He was only 62 when he died on January 14th 1993.

Ray and Charlie, birds of a feather

Charlie and Sarah take over (1993–2004)

I was in Pakistan when Ray died, coming back in April to find Charlie clearing out his room, dominated by a pea-green tile-work range. I grew up beside a similar one, of a gentler brown, in a house built in the first decade of the 20th century: it must have been the fashion when the Newmans took over. There was a shelf of polished brass shell cases and Charlie produced a box containing mint shillings of George II and George III. The last time they were out was when Alan Atkins visited and, by magic power, made them dance. Alan, with his intense look and some mystery in the air, was often in the Tap Room in the 1980s.

Changes started. On the negative side, Charlie was not particularly interested in shove ha'penny and darts; both teams faded away and only shove ha'penny revived. Jim & Philip Alexander, Charlie and, until his death, Ray played dominoes in the Tap Room. A game, Spoof, had a vogue, as did cribbage and backgammon. Often, Chris Foss, famous for his drawings in the sixties book, 'Joy of Sex', joined the games. The Christmas Draw, which Stella encouraged, finally fell from the calendar. But there was more music, including a Cajun group, The Boat Band, which turned up in May 1993 and afterwards. It drew in another group, The French Alligators. The furniture began to change that year, with the addition of a massive thin block of a Purbeck stone called grub from Trev Haysom's Worth Gate quarry. This is now a table beneath the inn sign. Nick Crutchfield's eccentric, yet surprisingly comfortable, driftwood armchair slipped into the Big Room.

In 1992, John and Nicky France took over Worth Craft Centre. Nicky became a very regular customer, the centre of a collection of younger folk, some of whom worked for her. Jack Daniels, already well known for his animal caricatures and about to launch on the local humans, started to drop in more often, sometimes with his two sons, Jake and Jaxon. So did Shirley Fielding and her lurcher, Buffy. As they reached eighteen and studenthood, the Caplestone Set – Annabel, Sophie and Emily Dean – invaded with friends, including Rob Besant (famous by proxy – his great aunt, Annie Besant, being important in India's Independence movement), Peter Du Cane, James Twist, Matt Moore, Helen Bray, Juliet and Leckie Haysom and their cousins, the Bibras. Some of that crew started to refer to the place as 'The Rumpus', which it was – when they were there!

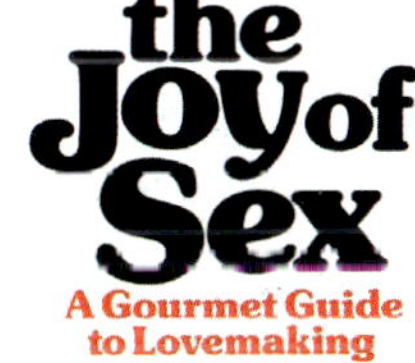

Artist Chris Foss

OPPOSITE
Charlie serving his apprenticeship

THE BOAT BAND WITH J C GALLOW

The Boat Band with LA Sheriff J.C. Gallow and right, The French Alligators

Jack Daniels' caricature of Big Sean Keeley

It was rarely quiet when Sean Keeley appeared. London Irish, big, blonde and handsome, he overcame agoraphobia by getting into a car and driving from North London till he hit the sea at Swanage. Usually accompanied by his guitar and a number of songs, he added his own 'Purbeck Song', a romantic ditty which invariably drew a groan. But he made people laugh. If he drove to The Square, he had to walk back. You knew he'd be walking when he sneezed; he sneezed on his third pint. One bitter New Year's Eve, his partner, Charlotte, set me the impossible task of delivering him home from The Square. I failed. He narrowly survived, being found beside the road at 6am

Julie Rooks, Jane Haw (who raised the Biggest Cow in Britain – a Charollais – at neighbouring Compact Farm); Juliet Begley (with or without daughter, Jessie), Karen Lyttle, Simon and Amanda all frequented the pub at this time. Like Mike Bizley, Hugh Sandall and the Quinns, they were among the late-evening folk at the pub; or were they early folk who stayed on? Gerry Burden joined the group in the corridor, as did Frances and Ian Taylor, whose son and daughter were fixtures, Roz marrying Jon James from Renscombe Farm. Late arrivals get a false impression of the clientele, rarely seeing people like Bill and Marion Norman or Nick and Liliana Mack, who, no less regular, come early in the evening. Perhaps Bill's son, Mark 'Nobby', does, too. He is certainly there late, along with his aged dog, Socks. Living nearby, people like him, Jeremy Hibbs or David and Richard Ralls can drop

in on impulse. There are other tipplers, like James Pembroke, who prefer Sunday lunchtimes. Hating to waste daylight hours, we used to refer to that slot as 'Rotten Row', mostly for Londoners.

Nicky France launched the brief reign of the Hat Club in 1995. John Taylor, then her tenant, bought a velvet smoking hat, complete with tassel, at Lamer Tree. That inspired her to produce a box full of eccentric hats; she, Charlie, Neil Harding, Jack Daniels, Derek O'Sullivan, John Taylor, Kevin Haine and Kevin Cross adopted such head pieces to appear at The Square each Sunday at 6pm. From there, they invaded other pubs and venues until the club faded out.

CLOCKWISE FROM TOP
The Square and Compass Hat Club: Johnny 'Two Prong' Taylor, 'Derelict' O'Sullivan, 'Little' Kevin Haine, Jack Daniels, Nicky France, Kevin Cross and Neil Harding

Billy Norman in The Corridor

On quieter winter evenings, the silence was shattered by an elderly wooden gramophone, fed from a huge, precarious stack of 78 rpm records, scavenged from the dump and Cottees sales. From time to time, they fell in an avalanche, always a few succumbing. Robeson, Caruso, Eddie Calvert, Vera Lynn, Richard Tauber. Some inspired us to sing along: 'Stormy Weather' was a favourite until it shattered! On one drunken evening, Charlie broke most of those records and fed the rest into the stove. The world moved on.

Sometimes there was unmusical cacophony in the Tap Room, like an evening in April 1991, when I listed 2 banjos, a tabla, a Jew's Harp, Mouth Organ and an accordion, producing 'joyous noise never approaching harmony or any recognisable tune.' On other evenings, Damian Viney joined in with his trombone, or Melissa Viney sang. It led to Band Night on Thursday, when Charlie declared that anything could be used as a musical instrument and encouraged everyone else to improvise. Amongst the less traditional instruments, he played neon tube light with polystyrene and drummed a large wooden barrel with two logs. Another fellow turned a Quality Street tin into a snare drum, whilst Nicky France made do with a comb and the empty plastic shell that had held Strepsils. Meanwhile, in the Big Room, Wendy Wharam started her story narrations. Inspired by The Rocky Horror Show, Cindy Prior might appear, gruesomely made up, with Steve Mason wearing black lipstick, eye-shadow and fishnet stockings to enhance the effect.

LEFT TO RIGHT
Mike Bizley, Ian Ching, Sarah Loudoun, Bacchus, Di Quinn, Cindy Prior, Steve Mason, Val Quinn, Charlie Newman, Billy Norman

Cindy, following the tradition of her parents, was often at The Square. She stood in behind the bar and always took an interest in anything that went on in the pub. Although she was much younger, she and Charlie were childhood friends, both using each other's home with freedom. Despite another age gap, she and Tilly Quinn became friends, involving themselves in some of the early Halloween dressing up sessions. Cindy was a constantly friendly presence in and out of the pub. Her sudden death on 11th July 2006, at a mere 32, came as a horrible blow. An indication of her popularity was the crowd that packed Worth Church for her funeral. The congregation flowed out across the churchyard. Afterwards, Charlie laid on food and drink for the mourners at The Square. Folk felt her absence at Square Fair, soon afterwards, but it was not her style to be a shadow over the future.

Nicky France's dog Jack

When Charlie Newman took up metal detecting, he classified his finds, in the face of 'treasure-hunting' criticisms, and soon became expert at telling the head of one Caesar from another. After full and new moons, when tides are lowest, he disappeared along the shore to excavate saurian remains. The beach could yield timbers of ancient wooden vessels, neatly dowled together, odd flotsam and jetsam, some of it valuable, the occasional corpse. He'd stagger up with what he could, surrounded by dogs – Shandy III, Abby, Fat Dog (a tough name to live with, but he grew tall, dark and handsome), Ben, Jake – most of them collies. When added to wandering dogs of visiting folk, the pub became overwhelmed by hounds, life interspersed with loud territorial conflicts. They were repelled by Cider and Guinness, two contemporary cats. Beasts almost took over the show. When Charlie and Sarah marked Fat Dog's 10th birthday, there were 20 canine guests.

Guinness

A cultural kidnapping took place in 1993. For eight years, Swanage Carnival included stone carving amongst its annual events. Val Quinn, Jonathan Sells, Charlie Newman were among those who carved there: it was an opportunity to make contacts and sell work. The sculptor, Mary Spencer Watson rounded it off with a drinks party at Dunshay Manor. The stone carving was neglected, so Val and others inspired Charlie to add it to Square Fair. The Haysoms, at St Aldhelm's Quarry, donated stone and carving became, and continues, an annual two-week event, starting at the end of July. The large Tyrannosaurus rex standing outside the pub was Val Quinn's contribution to that first stone-carving fortnight.

A shorn Shandy III

Mary Spencer Watson set her seal of approval by working a day at the first couple of stone fairs, and always dropping by each year afterwards. She continued her post-carving party, Charlie and Sarah contributing an increasing amount of the alcohol and effort. Her family, established at Dunshay since 1923, had stayed clear of local pub life but, coming to it late, she enjoyed taking apples up for the cider pressing day, or watching the autumn weigh-in of pumpkins. That Cider-making day didn't last long, but she and I took a load of apples up in October 1999. That evening, Sarah tried to persuade me to drink cider. I refused, but she persisted. Finally, I agreed so long as she took the same price as Eileen charged when I first came up – tenpence. She acquiesed, although she ripped me off, charging 10P, not Eileen's 10d.

CLOCKWISE FROM BELOW

The sculptor, Mary Spencer Watson; Jim Davis at the original Swanage stone carving; Charlie with his work; Marion Norman and Val Quinn debating Stalin; and poster by Ian Ching

The
Square & Compass
Stone Carving Festival

Worth Matravers
Dorset. BH19 3LF

CLOCKWISE FROM ABOVE

Val Quinn with T-Rex; the railway carriage guest house arrives – yesteryear's homes, many locals were born in them; poster by Ian Ching; Stone Carving postcard featuring: Jonathan Sells, Tony Pilot, Ian Ching, Val Quinn, Jim and Stan Bonfield

Early scales

Another annual event, Pumpkin Day, seems to have started in 1996. Once installed in the calendar for early October, it flourished, although, by the end of the day, only the successful grower remembered the triumphant weight of his pumpkin. Examples of the victors are Alan Smith's meek 204lb in 1997, Paul Loudoun's 468 lb in 2001 and Ray Aplin's 460 lb in 2003. A 776lb monster grown by the Baggs family of Worgret in 2006 made Charlie's spring-balance redundant: its limit was 600lb. The winner is auctioned for charity. At the first Pumpkin Days, Dave Eyles acted as compare; a role he took on Burns Night, too. Later, Andy and Becky Wells started to turn up from Devon to help out then, as well as at Square Fair. Those vast golden pumpkins that slowly sag in front of the pub as autumn progresses are not alone. There are also quirky little oddities, or conservative gourds forced into strange erotic poses. Bale-tossing and scarecrow competitions have crept in, and inevitably there is music in the evening.

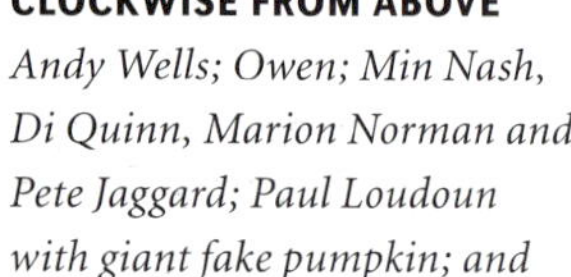

CLOCKWISE FROM ABOVE
Andy Wells; Owen; Min Nash, Di Quinn, Marion Norman and Pete Jaggard; Paul Loudoun with giant fake pumpkin; and auctioneer Ward Bullock

CLOCKWISE FROM ABOVE
Karla's kitchen; Charlie; Pumpkin Day crowd; Kevin Hunt ; and one of the winners, Charlie's uncle Alan Smith

CLOCKWISE FROM ABOVE
'Nobby' Norman; gourds for sale; Cath and MC Andy; Paul Loudoun's accomplished carving; and the Bale Tossing competition

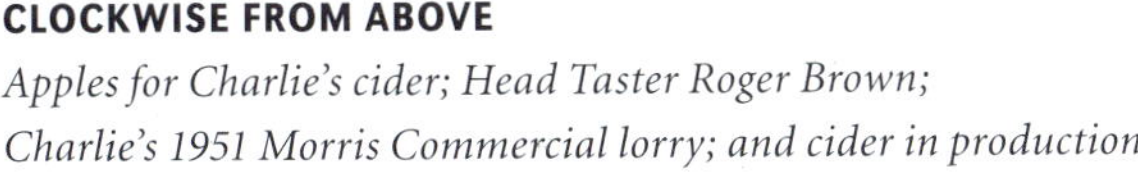

CLOCKWISE FROM ABOVE

Apples for Charlie's cider; Head Taster Roger Brown; Charlie's 1951 Morris Commercial lorry; and cider in production

Charlie's submarine-like cider vat

Martin Hanley washing the apples

CLOCKWISE FROM RIGHT

The Beard Festival: 'Traveller' Will, Gary and partner Becky, bar manager Janet, Poppy-Joy Daniels and Jean; and below Charlie's stainless steel hydraulic cider press;

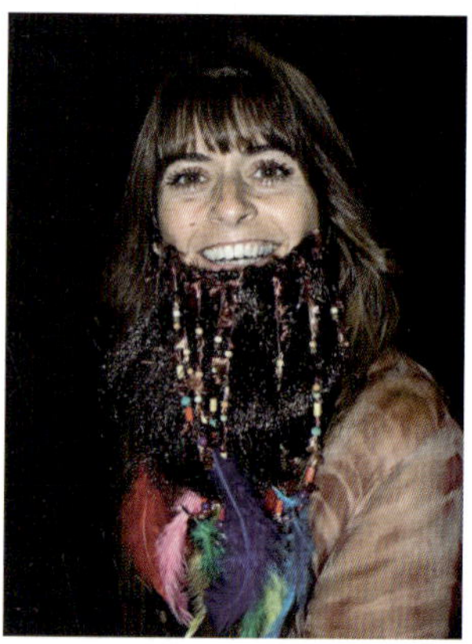

Burn's Night joined the calendar under Charlie's tenure, celebrated with a generous flow of whisky and a surfeit of tartan. The 'wee timorous beastie', the haggis, wanders even this far south. In 2007 it was a neat display of Charlie's generosity, with a hefty haggis meal for everyone. Stephen Devlin, 'Vo', gave a lively recital of Robbie's more risqué verse, followed by Richard Smith, with his sharply humorous poems.

Quite apart from regular invasions by the leather and heavy bike brigade, some customers turn up in odd vehicles. A retired army officer, Major Ian Crompton, and his wife, Betty, had a choice; they would drive up from Swanage in either their red or their blue 1920s Austin. A neat man, sometimes sporting a spotted cravat, as regional representative of the British Legion, Ian was generous in his efforts to help ex-servicemen. Nick Mack, clad in wartime biking gear, sometimes rides up on his 1946 Ariel. One afternoon, six spotless 1960s Austin A35s were parked outside. The Newmans took their part. In the 1930s, Old Charlie had a much-sought-after three-wheeled Morgan, which ended its life in a quarry hole near Acton. In 1992, Young Charlie bought a blue 1951 Morris Commercial lorry. It worked hard for its living, taking friends down to Chapmans Pool and supplying outdoor bars at fetes and weddings. Later, he acquired a smart bi-coloured 1953 AC saloon. In 2000, Pete Du Cane and I talked of biking back from India. Charlie, fresh back from a trip to New Zealand, promised a barrel of beer if we succeeded. One drizzly September lunchtime, we rode in, fresh from Rajasthan, on a 1962 Enfield 350cc. Useless mechanics, we had no real trouble all the way but, after a pint at The Square, could we get that bloody bike to start?

Highland Queen was Ray's favourite tipple

Major Ian Crompton's 1920s Austin

Richard Smith aka Elvis McGonagall, poet and armchair revolutionary, 2007 Burns night

Peter Du Cane and Ilay at Dunshay Manor before India road trip

Pretty Purbeck is a good setting for filming, so crews with cameras turn up. These days, as its fame spreads, the pub is often the target, but there are other films which choose it for a scene or two. Part of 'Nuts in May', directed by Mike Leigh and featured as 'Play for the Day' on BBC TV, was shot in the Big Room in 1975. One evening, when they were shooting 'Wilde' in 1996, I sat, work-soiled, in the Tap Room as gayer members of the cast tried, unsuccessfully, to persuade two young farmers to their way of thinking. Tom Baker, 'Dr Who', visited the pub whilst filming an episode at Winspit in the late 1970s and 'The Mayor of Casterbridge' used the pub as a location for two weeks, adjusting the facade and shooting in both rooms. The mayor was 'interred' just in front, but his headstone is now behind The Scott Arms, Kingston. There are more tenuous connections with the medium: the film maker and historian, Kevin Brownlow, who came to The Square as a boy, cherishes his photo sitting on the wall.

Dr Who at Winspit

The print media are always using The Square for copy. In March 1996, 'You' magazine published a piece by Terence Conran's son, Tom, a restaurateur. He lists The Square in his 'Address Book Secrets': 'I love the old-fashioned atmosphere. It's like an extension of someone's house.' Sadly, he doesn't mention the haute cuisine.

In May 1994, the fate of The Square and Compass was sealed. One evening, with Nikki Hann with her guitar and three guys playing Irish-style music in the Big Room, Charlie announced "I bought the pub last Tuesday" before launching into a rough-house, with Neil, Sarah and Charlie throwing and receiving buckets of water. Kevin Cross, straight from work and looking dapper, walked into one bucketful. On 21st June, Charlie called in all the regulars for a free drink or five to celebrate the purchase. There was music, of course, with Rui Ribeiro among the performers. Stan Bonfield plied me with whiskies until I staggered home in the early hours, leaving the music still playing. Few people have a clear vision of that night.

As owners, it was now worth Charlie and Sarah embarking on all the improvements the brewers had left in abeyance. Ray Bray and Neil Harding, with assistance from Charlie and others, were soon hard at work on the building. It was replumbed and rewired, two new kitchens put in and the upstairs living quarters renovated. There was a lavatorial renaissance, too. The Ladies, long situated at the back of the building (where it boasted a seat painted by Di Quinn with a ring of alligator's teeth), now lies seductively beside the Gents. When completed, Bill Norman cut a scarlet ribbon.

Neil and Charlie receive a soaking

The old gent(s), Les Travers

Under Charlie's regime, a museum became the graceful fulfilment of his father's original scheme. Open to all, it was completed in 1998 in the projecting wing, the end of which had been partitioned off by Raymond in the mid 1970s as a Children's Room. A museum is an odd feature for a rural pub, but it satisfies many years effort, housing Raymond's and Young Charlie's collections. Mary added to it, seeking out fossils near Punfield Cove, where, on one outing, she took a fine photograph of her father's favourite bird, a peregrine falcon. Display cases were made by Hugh Sandall, Ray Bray and Bill Cook. Lee Willment also helped, and Karen Lyttle wrote out captions. The exhibits include Jurassic and Cretaceous molluscs, fish and dinosaur remains, prehistoric artefacts, pre-Roman and Roman coinage and jewellery and more recent objects. Trappings from the Halsewell wreck were gifted by divers, amongst them cannonballs and Spanish silver coins overprinted with George III.

CLOCKWISE FROM LEFT

Jon 'Baz' Foot's dry stone 'Egg'; and with Karen Lyttle bumper car racing

OPPOSITE

David Clarke's 'Da Vinci's Man' from 1991, assisted by Val Quinn

Securiscare guarding the precious things of the Museum

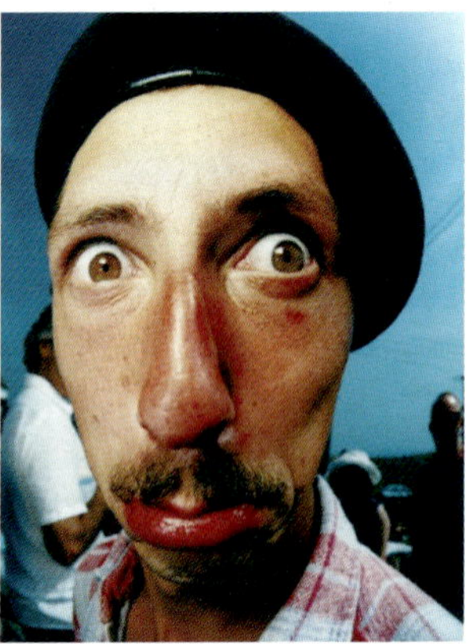

Pronghorn and Charlie

Naughty punters once added a non-Square pasty to the fossils. Charlie, inspired by a briefly-fashionable work of art, put a fresh chicken turd, labelled 'hot and steamy, aged 1 hour' into one case beside rather older ones of dinosaurs and ancient fish.

If Charlie's tenure is memorable for any one thing, it is Music. He has taken a great interest in the groups going around, playing. He welcomes and encourages anyone who comes by with a musical instrument or talent. Often, towards the end of the evening, he joins the players on accordion or tea-chest. He supported Brian Cockerell's interest in folk music and, for many years, Thursday became folk night. This, after fading away, has been revived. The Square has become a recognised stage for groups touring Britain, but local talent continues to feature. In summer, Morris dancers perform in front of the pub. A good group, The Dead Plants, settled

in the parish; they perform at The Square when not further afield. And the famous Repetitive Concertina Player still drops by. Complaints of noise persist, a living tradition since the eighteenth century. The oldest example, still cherished, is a letter, dated 20th June 1939, from the brewer concerning Mrs Oliver of Compass Cottage, who was particularly harassed at weekends in the summer months.

Charlie didn't confine himself to music. In September 2002, having worked behind the bar all summer, Juliet Haysom asked if she could show her latest drawings in the Big Room. He agreed, so, for three days in September, the usual décor disappeared in favour of her 37 exhibits. A pioneering success, she sold 18 drawings, credit going to her skill as well as the venue!

There are the logistics of keeping the show on the road. If Charlie was the entertainer, the free spirit who kept the pub attractive, he relied on Sarah. She curbed the excesses, steered the place approximately within Britain's archaic licensing laws, took on cooking and kept the house orderly. Her part in the success of The Square didn't bring her fair praise, but it was with her backing that Charlie succeeded. In October, she would hold her well-merited birthday party in a marquee in front of the pub.

There was a change in the bar staff. In the vacations, the student set included Sophie Dean, Juliet and Leckie Haysom, Hester Viney, Lilian Handy, John Blakeley and Yewande. Juliet liked Charlie's favourite remark on busy summer days: "Roll on January!" Sarah's nephew, Jamie Hannant and his partner, Marie Seavor

Marie Seavor; Jamie Hannant and Charlie; Anna Bibra, Sophie Dean and Charlie with the Chapmans cow

CLOCKWISE FROM RIGHT

Paul Bradley, who played Nigel Bates in 'Eastenders', sings with 'H Kipper'; an original 1939 letter from the brewery enquiring of noise complaints from Compass Cottage – no change there!; Roger Brown relaxes; 'Little' Kevin Haine; Charlie with his squeezebox

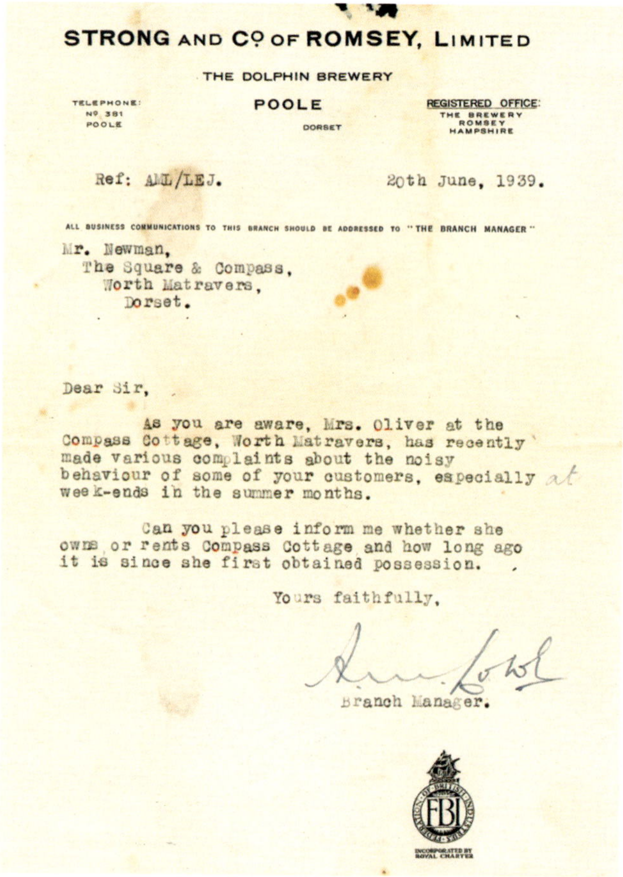

STRONG AND Co. OF ROMSEY, LIMITED

THE DOLPHIN BREWERY

TELEPHONE: No. 381 POOLE — POOLE DORSET — REGISTERED OFFICE: THE BREWERY ROMSEY HAMPSHIRE

Ref: AML/LEJ. 20th June, 1939.

ALL BUSINESS COMMUNICATIONS TO THIS BRANCH SHOULD BE ADDRESSED TO "THE BRANCH MANAGER"

Mr. Newman,
The Square & Compass,
Worth Matravers,
Dorset.

Dear Sir,

As you are aware, Mrs. Oliver at the Compass Cottage, Worth Matravers, has recently made various complaints about the noisy behaviour of some of your customers, especially at week-ends in the summer months.

Can you please inform me whether she owns or rents Compass Cottage and how long ago it is since she first obtained possession.

Yours faithfully,

Branch Manager.

FBI
INCORPORATED BY ROYAL CHARTER

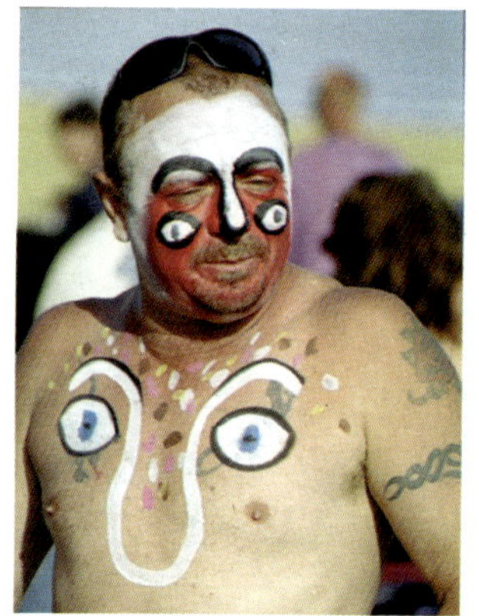

CLOCKWISE FROM LEFT

Charlie, Rob Besant and Jamie Hannant reconstruct 'The Bystander'; Charlie's half-desert island bedroom at White Lodge; and the pub team celebrating winning one of many awards

Spinner and weaver Deidre Baines

took an increasing part in running the pub. Occasionally, the younger set, along with Charlie, brought a novel artistic slant to the region, creating a spectacular if ephemeral driftwood cow, complete with litre milk-bottle udders, on Chapmans Pool beach. On winter evenings Sarah, Liliana Mack, Frankie Taylor and Deidre started wool weaving in the Big Room. The wheel turned and new faces appeared behind the bar, including Jack & Jenny Cockerell, (whose parents also served in their time), Richard and Helen Smith, Max Mumford, Janet O'Kane and Emma, her daughter, most of whom continued when Kevin Hunt took over. Charlie's cousin, Dave Harris, remains, too, with his choice of sixties music. Occasionally, he has run the pub.

There was a nice misunderstanding in the Tap Room one evening. A group of friendly Travellers were chatting when a Posh Lady came in. She had camping experience, so they launched into travel talk and places to stop en route. The lady said "Of course, the joints are not what they were." She looked puzzled at the jovial agreement.

The Square's exposed position is fine to witness the Elements. Every clear night, the debate resumes as to whether the lights of Cherbourg, occasionally clearly visible, are a real image or a reflection from the atmosphere. Benfield, in 'Purbeck Shop', answered, correctly, that the earth's curvature makes reality impossible. But the lights are visible, nevertheless, and your mobile phone knows you are in France! The pub overlooked a white world and was besieged by snow in 1947 and again in 1963. Ian Ching arrived in Worth as a boy in time for the snow drifts of early 1978, which also blocked the roads. I was caught at St Aldhelm's Quarry, where roofs fell in. In 1999, folk who watched the near-total eclipse from St Aldhelm's Head or at Swyre Head turned up for a drink afterwards, a guy playing a harp in the background! The pub is a great vantage point for watching thunderstorms cruising up the Channel. A magnificent one passed in June 2005, the day before Kevin Hunt's 50th birthday celebrations. Divine fireworks? Sadly, meteor showers tend to streak behind the building.

In the early 2000s, Charlie began to talk of retreat, leaving the pub in the hands of a manager. Simultaneously, he embarked on designing and building a new house on the site of Channel View. When planners doubted whether there had been a dwelling on the site, Reg Prior was able to prove that he was born there! A lot of Square regulars took part in the construction. Neil Harding did most of the construction work, helped by Dave Evans, Jake Jackson, Ray Bray & Kevin Hunt (timberwork

of the roof), Hugh Sandall (more woodwork, including the fine stairway). Alistair Bowerman concentrated on the decoration and I cut the stone paving for the floor, which Neil laid. Later, Toby Wiggins painted the archaic mural on the slope of the ceiling. Charlie and Sarah held one of their excellent parties as a house-warming on the last day of November 2003.

Young Charlie had always planned to build an ideal house but, oddly, without the idea of moving into it: that came as an afterthought! As it developed, he was distracted from the pub. Sarah more or less took over the logistics, then Jamie Hannant and Marie Seavor agreed to devote themselves to the place for a year. Gradually, that year overran, and Jamie was offered other, attractive work. Already settled in Worth and having worked on the new Channel View, Kevin Hunt became a natural choice to take over management of The Square.

Channel View - the site of Charlie's new house

Under the new regime, Charlie and Sarah were increasingly free and found themselves going in different directions. Conducting one's private life in a public space is always difficult, but eventually Charlie started a new relationship with Cath Bradshaw, an actress. She combines a successful acting career with bar work, enjoying the environment but steering clear of the business. What with liking music, singing and playing the guitar, she fits in well. Sarah is now happily married to Gordon Foot, but maintains contact with The Square, still cooking pasties & sausage pie.

Now, Charlie and Cath, settled into the new house, are retreating from the everyday concerns of the pub. After years in the spotlight, both cherish a more private life, devoting time to vegetables, chickens and other farming projects. They have bought more land nearby. After all, Charlie's ancestors, both the Newmans and Smiths, were involved in agriculture, so mud as well as beer is in the blood.

Charlie and Cath dressed for '40s style film night, 2006

Kevin Hunt manages

In autumn 2003, Kevin Hunt launched energetically into full time management of The Square. He entered the place ten years previously, when helping Neil Harding build a cottage for Brian Cockerell. He had met Brian at craft fairs, where Kevin sold his painted animal portraits. (Charlie acquired two: of Fat Dog, and of the pony, Winston). He came from Malvern, connected with Worth as the town to which the Radar establishment shifted in 1942, and flies the flag of tradition by keeping chickens and dogs (he has two). Even the bike, a Motoguzzi SP 1000, is not a real breach; after all, Raymond had motorbikes.

Naturally, management changes the story. A manager doesn't have the freedom of an owner. Kevin maintains the high standard of drink and aims to keep The Square "the sort of pub that I'd like to be in." He has introduced a table-tennis championship, held in late Autumn and early Spring, and tries to convert folk to his hobby of sea kayaking. He is as keen as Charlie on the sound environment, but turns more towards World music.

Winston and, below, Fat Dog by Kevin Hunt

Truckstop Honeymoon, the band

Kevin decided to bring in a smoking ban in July 2006, although not fanatically anti-smoking, to see what affect it had on trade before it becomes mandatory in July 2007. The Square has always been a smokey pub, yet the ban doesn't seem to have worried many folk. They have got used to it, and the non-smoking nature attracts the ardently smokeless.

The beer still flows. Life rolls on, with more singing, dancing, laughing, perhaps a little weeping as each in turn drops from the perch. Amongst loyal regulars, the Famous flit by, uproars come and go. Every summer Square Fair and the Stone Carving flourish, usually blessed by the weather but Mary Spencer Watson's death, in March 2006, brought an end to her annual drinks party. The Square is more a thing of flesh and blood than of stone and mortar. The People make the Pub. Charlie wants to thank all those People.

★

So March 2007 marks a Newman Century at The Square and Compass. In 1907 'Old' Charlie and Florence Newman moved into an isolated village pub, barely known in Purbeck. Under their tenure, with Charlie's skill as an astute businessman and a natural entertainer, aided by Florence's ability to run a kitchen and a husband, it became popular. Together, they reigned for forty-six years, lifting the pub to prominence. For almost twenty years, Eileen Newman kept the ship on course, later helped and hindered by Frank, whose ship went off course. Raymond and Stella Newman took over. Raymond, over twenty years, kept his hand gently on the tiller, preserving the character of the place and encouraging its quirky nature. He was supported by Mary Newman, then by Sarah and Charlie Newman. When they took over, 'Young' Charlie Newman finally bought the place and filled it with more music, cherishing its spirit, while Sarah, applying the brakes of commonsense, kept the vessel clear of rocks for eleven years. Now, Charlie and Kevin Hunt trim the sails for the next hundred years. They'll probably keep to sails. Who wants another fibre-glass gin-palace?

OPPOSITE
Old Charlie Newman and brother George

"Ladies and gentlemen…
…last orders at the bar if you please!"

Bibliography

Benfield, Eric, 1935 Peter Davies, London, *Bachelor's Knap*; Benfield, Eric, 1990 Ensign Publications, Southampton, *Purbeck Shop*; Hooke, Nina Warner, 1989 Chiver Press, Bath, *Seal Summer*; Latham, Colin & Stobbs, Anne, 1999 Sutton Publishing Ltd, Stroud, *Pioneers of Radar*; Pushman, David, 1999, Downsway Books, *The Loss of the SS Treveal*; Wallace, Marjorie, 1986, *That's the way it was...*

Illustration credits

Page 7
Newman Family Archive
Page 8
Source unknown
Page 9
Newman Family Archive;
David Pushman
Page 10
Jack Daniels Archive;
Penny Brooke
Page 11
E.C. Pascoe Holman
Page 12
Maps: Dorset History Centre;
Photos: David Haysom
Page 13
Jim Chambers
Page 14
Jack Daniels Archive
Page 15
Leon Heron
Page 16
Basil Stumpe;
Leon Heron
Page 17
Jack Daniels Archive
Page 18
John Doust, ARPS
Page 19
Newman Family Archive;
Richard & Prue Bedwell;
Basil Stumpe
Page 20
Tereska Roe
Page 22
Dorset History Centre
Page 25
Newman Family Archive
Page 26
Dorset History Centre
Page 30
Smith Family Archive;
Jack Daniels Archive
Page 31
Jack Daniels Archive
Page 32
Public Records Office
Page 33
Newman Family Archive
Page 34
Drawn by James Twist
Page 36
Newman Family Archive
Page 37
Bournemouth Echo;
Newman Family Archive
Page 39
Newman Family Archive
Page 40
Jack Daniels Archive;
Newman Family Archive
Page 41
Newman Family Archive;
Lloyds News
Page 42
Newman Family Archive
Page 43
MOD,
Newman Family Archive
Page 46
Newman Family Archive
Page 47
Newman Family Archive;
Postcard unmarked
Page 48
Glasgow School of Art
Page 49
Newman Family Archive:
Augustus John;
Daily Mail
Page 50
Newman Family Archive:
David Low
Leslie Moffat Ward
Page 51
Newman Family Archive
Pages 52-53
Newman Family Archive
Pages 54-55
Newman Family Archive:
'Beck';
Newman Family Archive
Page 56
Rhoda Bower;
Pat Welsh;
Newman Family Archive
Page 57
Newman Family Archive:
F. Paterson;
Postcard: R.A.P. Co. Ltd.,
London EC1
John Crabb Family Archive
Page 60
Jack Daniels Archive;
Denys Watkins-Pitchford,
courtesy of David Higham
Associates, from Eric Benfield's
book 'Southern English'
Page 61
Daily Mirror;
F. Copeland
Page 62
Newman Family Archive;
The People
Page 63
Newman Family Archive;
Postcard unmarked
Page 64
Courtesy Pat Welsh,
photographer unknown
Page 65
Western Gazette;
Jo Lawrence, photographer
unknown;
Newman Family Archive:
Sillinger Studios, Wien
Page 66
Newman Family Archive
Page 67
Newman Family Archive;
Elliott Seabrooke;
F. Copeland
Pages 68-69
Newman Family Archive
Page 70
Postcard unmarked
Page 71
Leon Heron
Pages 72-73
Newman Family Archive:
photographer unknown (BBC)
Page 75
Newman Family Archive:
Murray Hardy, Leyland Paint &
Varnish Co.
Page 76
Newman Family Archive
Page 77
TRE (MOD)
purbeckradar.org.uk
Page 78
Worth Archive;
Newman Family Archive;
TRE (MOD)
purbeckradar.org.uk
Page 79
Jack Daniels Family Archive;
Newman Family Archive
Page 80
John Gilson
Page 81
Rhoda Bower;
Sketch by John Gilson
Page 82
Newman Family Archive;
Joan Muspratt
Page 83
Mary Dwen (née Newman);
Postcard unmarked;
Newman Family Archive

Pages 84-85
Newman Family Archive;
Sasha
Page 86
Rhoda Bower;
Newman Family Archive;
Page 88
The Daily Graphic
Page 89
Newman Family Archive
Page 90
Brian Stumpe;
Newman Family Archive
Page 91
Brian Stumpe;
Viney Family Archive
Page 93
Newman Family Archive
Page 94
Brian Stumpe
Page 95
Newman Family Archive;
Jim Chambers
Pages 96-97
Newman Family Archive
Page 98
Newman Family Archive
Page 99
Brian Stumpe;
Pat Welsh
Page 100
Basil Stumpe;
Brian Stumpe
Page 101
Newman Family Archive
Page 103
Alan Smith & Family Archive
Page 104
Newman Family Archive
Page 105
Biff Crabbe
Page 106
Newman Family Archive
Page 107
Newman Family Archive;
Margaret Kirkwood;
Gerald Corbett
Page 108
Gerald Corbett;
Chris Foss

Page 109
Jim Chambers;
Socks: Victoria Cross
Page 111
Gerald Corbett
Pages 112-113
Newman Family Archive
Pages 114-115
Jim Chambers;
Newman Family Archive
Pages 116-117
Quinn Family Archive;
Newman Family Archive
Page 118
Rachel Timings
Page 119
Jack Daniels Archive
Page 120
Jack Daniels Archive;
Tereska Roe;
Sheila Ballantyne
Page 121
Gerald Corbett;
Tereska Roe;
Newman Family Archive
Pages 122-123
Jack Daniels Archive
Page 124
Quinn Family Archive
Page 125
Newman Family Archive
Page 126
Gerald Corbett
Page 127
Chris Foss
Page 128
The Boat Band;
The French Alligators;
Jack Daniels Archive
Pages 129
Jack Daniels Archive
Pages 130
Tereska Roe
Jack Daniels Archive
Pages 131
Newman Family Archive;
Jack Daniels Archive:
courtesy Getty Images

Page 132
Quinn Family Archive;
Poster: Ian Ching
Page 133
Quinn Family Archive;
Newman Family Archive;
Poster: Ian Ching
Page 134
Jack Daniels Archive;
George Crane;
Newman Family Archive
Page 135
Jack Daniels Archive;
Robin Eva;
George Crane;
Newman Family Archive
Page 136
Martin Hanley;
Robin Eva;
Martin Hanley;
Robin Eva;
Tom Raphael Eaves
Page 137
Jack Daniels Archive
Page 138
Jack Daniels Archive;
Martin Hanley
Page 139
George Crane;
Joss Barratt
Page 140
Jack Daniels Archive;
Dr Who, BBC
Page 141
Newman Family Archive
Page 142
Jack Daniels Archive:
Art by David Clarke
Page 143
Jack Daniels Archive;
Lyttle Archive
Page 144
Jack Daniels Archive;
Pronghorn
Page 145
Newman Family Archive;
George Crane

Page 146
Newman Family Archive;
Jack Daniels Archive;
George Crane;
Karla Joy Cherryjackdaniels;
Page 147
Gerald Corbett;
Newman Family Archive:
The Daily Telegraph/Abbot Ale
Award photographer unnamed
Pages 148-149
Newman Family Archive
Page 150
Newman Family Archive
Page 151
Truckstop Honeymoon;
Drawings, Kevin Hunt
Page 153
Newman Family Archive:
Page 156
Swanage Directory, 1934,
courtesy Ray Aplin

Beer mats: private collection, with respect to all illustrators, photographers, companies and manufacturers.

Where possible we have sought throughout this project to seek permissions for the wonderful illustrations contained within these pages. We will be happy to include any corrections or missing acknowledgements in any future reprints.